THE NIGHT BEFORE LAST

Richard Chaffer

Cover design by LeFroste exclusively for
EOD by graphic artist Giovanni Duenas
Library of Congress
Cataloging-in-Publishing Data
Chaffer, Richard (1952-)
Printed in the United States of America

ISBN 978-0-9831185-0-3

To My Family

I have full cause of weeping, but this heart
shall break into a hundred thousand flaws.
Or ere I'll weep. O fool! I shall go mad.

Shakespeare

King Lear

Part One

I

I arrived in town with no more than a satchel and a sleeping bag. I would suppose that it was no less nor more than any other sleepy seaside town. However, it seemed from the outset to; perhaps, garnish the promises of my becoming a writer. I was on the verge of a happiness that I never before knew.

In the start it seemed as though everyone had crossed my path to bid me hello. Favorable beginnings you might say. Auspicious indeed! The truth be known I was walking proudly with my head pointed toward the sky and nothing in sight to prevent me from the vanity that followed me.

It was only time before I was permitted to ride on the right track. Only time which would not forsaken me to scribble as best I could. Yes, I would bleed freely opening new horizons to catch the spring rain and there with a moments pause I would matriculate with the best of them. What brave stories would bully me to the conclusion of my tall tales of sustenance, groping for a dramatic substance that would entitle me to publication. It was as good as gold and I wouldn't shrink from the task at hand.

At home the windows in the kitchenette struck me at once. Nonetheless it wasn't necessarily a curse. Later I spoke and said: I give my heart, oh, this sun of gold, but the eternal echoes by the sea have me by the collar. I cried out loud from within but my voice wasn't heard. It was with invisibility that I crowed. And, by god man, there were people everywhere! All about me a fury of sound and motion. And so, by consequence, I fled down one block and up the next bent on eluding these rascals at my side.   Whether or not it was the spring rain, well, I couldn't be certain but everyone seemed to don an umbrella. That much was undeniable. By now I had only sheltered myself with a newspaper. By any token it wasn't a hard rain.

Soon it would be summer and I had no new plans with which to curse these adherents of the surreal. I found myself staring out of my window at the cars streaming past me. I discovered that there were more white cars than not and I wondered if this wasn't some sign of sorts to convey my plight. Sometimes I would stare so long, racking up the many possibilities that it nearly brought me to tears. Daft with the plausible as though a shroud had fallen upon me I would pledge to write a better book than one could imagine.

Things, I was sure, would pick up! After all I was to these daunting others a senior and I could easily impart with rapture that which presented itself. But today was different! There were icons of great doubt festering at my brow as I brought these blackguards and rebels to rest. How long could one wander without remorse at these beginnings. Stymied by these fits and starts I hunkered down oblivious of their trespasses.

That night, in its very midst, I took to gasping for air. I opened the window and peered outside to draw my breath but nothing came of it. I was on the verge of tears, my fists clenched to catch my breath but no matter how hard I tried I couldn't remedy my condition nor my despair. Instead I was forced to hack up phlegm and to seize the moment wherein I might capture the freedom of breathing once again. And meanwhile I was scratching like a monkey. Time passed and as I was spent nearly crying for air I finally fell to sleep where I lay comatose for the remainder of the night.

The haze of the sun awoken me at the nape of my neck. I nearly prayed for solace to these terms of my struggle. Above me soared the birds cracking the hulls of nuts on the rooftops and frolicking up and down. My tears, momentarily, have made way to splendor. The moon, oh, but to hold you close. But were these writings merely ramshackle prose? Sometimes, often in fact, it was enough to make you lose your mind. Was it too long winded or was it beyond reproach? Was I wasting my time? But, in part, what matters has been settled by this unrestrained rage. Was I crying rivers? A fat chance, monsieur. But must I shout! I told myself. For crying out loud, man, was I nothing more than an idle fool rubbing the sleep from his eyes. My hideous plight was no more than observing secretly the goings-on about me. Why had I turned out to be this freak of nature? I was the object seen through a spy hole. Still, I had conducted myself in as chivalrous of a mood that I knew how. Despite the weather of this f, the mechanical behavior of these imps and the surliness that begot them, I was well on my way, not merely crawling, to the rhythms of these proceedings.

Perhaps what I needed was a night of saturnalia where it is only becoming to strip down and fornicate to one's desire. However, not given to such a scene of an orgy, let alone a frosted kiss upon the temples of the awaiting succubus, I endured. Why doesn't anyone come forth on my behalf? What spears await me in the hallways of this madness? Meanwhile I try. It is my nature. Should I permit this foreign element to apprehend me? Why of course not, I thought to myself. My lot was to pounce upon an idea no matter how feeble. If I was to make a wish would I not forgive and forget those that preceded me? But by now my pants were baggy and my sleeves were threadbare and this lurid silence was sowing the seeds of doubt. It was merely a day's work, I exclaimed. For I had come, by now, to wreak havoc with those unfortunate enough to cross my path. Gritting my teeth I took to a formidable stance worthy of the most fastidious soul. And there I stood arms akimbo. Such occasions were meant to be exploited. After all, otherwise, wasn't I searching for a reprieve that didn't exist?

By now it was quite clear that I was

both being watched and listened to as though I was an experiment of sorts. I was flexing and staring for an aperture, camera ready. Still I was forced to unearth any clues to this imprisonment. It was, meanwhile, agreed unto myself that I would conduct myself with due dignity. No matter how desperate and urgent the circumstances fight and flight wouldn't desert me. The stage upon which I was stationed was a destiny unheard of in all of these trying times. However, I pursued my plight with great vim and vigor. Sometimes I was startled by my lack of discretion in the secretive manners that abound around me. On the other hand it was not without tears that I sometimes succumbed to these villains. At such times I could feel my blood boil and at the same time the tears would flow freely. So I was spent and not worthy of my post as a watchman nor the developer of tall tales.

Nonetheless I struggled for an approbation that would keep me going for the duration of time ill spent with these fantastic hordes of my followers or as I better called them, in jest, my dear miscreants. But for now the candlelight is going out, extinguished, and I am left in the dark, left alone to scuttle among the eaves of this paltry creation. However was I whining now, merely chomping at the bit? Or was I above these colossal terms moving each way then far standing above these roses, perched for good carrion. Should I simmer from these blasts of heat and the blowing wind? Please, call off these hound dogs!

Meanwhile the sun rose once again. I awoke in my street clothes as so many times before and hobbled to the bathroom. After relieving myself I took my seat at the desk. I was thinking, once upon a time, how easy it was to merely live. Now I lay in exile awaiting any elopement from this poverty and this chase. All scrutiny was presently at my beck and call. I was well aware that those surrounding me were time and time again the same people and I was beginning to hold a grudge. Why, oh why, were these rebels so very repugnant? Could we not get along?

Stepping out of my little room I wondered all the while who were the plaintiffs and the defendants in this desperate trial. I roamed and waited and slept at long intervals in silence on a park bench until darkness finally fell upon me. However, I didn't rave nor rant as the day before and, all in all, I felt a certain satisfaction as these fates conspired against me.

At home I tore into my book with a vengeance. It appeared that I was drunk with this flapdoodle that I expelled with such great ease. Whether it was rubbish or not didn't seem to matter although most certainly I would deposit it neatly into the trash tomorrow. If all of my instincts were going to hell didn't I owe this mischief to myself despite its contrariness. Always looking where to go I find myself lost more than not. Hmmm, call me a fool, I said to myself, but these doldrums have me under the weather. I can feel it in my bones!

I was feeling low but not enough so to deter me from my true post. No, I wouldn't hear of it! Should I succumb to these unruly voices would mean sure death and I wasn't used up quite yet. Should all motives go straight to hell, so be it. To embrace these mischief makers I could not do.

The town clock struck twelve noon and I lay out a curse for this mortal reminder. In my mind I was always spent going forward, never backward. At the same time was I possessed? I say this with some determination and I scowl.

In the mail I received correspondence stating 'keep this for your records' and I laughed to beat hell. At home an argument ensued next door and I watched very carefully at their porch through the fish-eye lens on the door. But I wasn't about to draw pistols nor any such heroics. Instead it was merely like a sneeze and nothing more.

Nevertheless this sad and sorry business was taking its toll. Indeed what was once upon a time my gladness paled in the face of these thoughts and words. So much time had passed but I was no more closer to the hour of delivery of this plaintive soul.

Oh, my dear man, with my last coins I took a bus to be around people and to transport myself back down town. I was, again, without any company in sight and I couldn't very well drum up any new prospects in this late hour. Mark my words! Insanity poured over me. I read the menu outside the entrance door and pondered my meal. It was the one for which I had no money. Through the baize door I entered the restaurant bent on having a last meal before I was arrested.

At my meal I nearly wept as I sat among those well off and myself in such ruins. I was surprised that they had permitted me entrance being in such a state of squalor. Soon people would be talking about my lonesome appearance as I would attempt to glide out of the premises. I was timing the entrance and presence of the waiter to decide upon my departure. Glad to be done with it I finally lurched outside the door and scrambled down the street.

What, to be sure, would insulate me from these abhorrent others. There was nothing to be done about it!

My eyes had grown watery and, again, I had no place to go. As I had sold my coat some few days ago I was shivering from the cold and damp. For the pittance received I was now suffering from the sell of it and I decided to stuff my sweatshirt with newspapers.

It dawned on me, with a full belly from the food, that I might now be introduced to some of the players in this game and volley. As a result I stuck out my thumb. Yes, it was time to share in this fund of knowledge. It seemed like ages before I was picked up and I welcomed it to no end. A rather comical looking character pulled over. I immediately sensed his plight balancing these rather unforgivable circumstances with my fate.

'Hello, my dear friend' I rallied. He simply nodded, not going out of his way with any acts of friendliness. But I was quick to discover this snake oil. I was riding with the occult, anxious to meet one of these operatives in this chase that had so entirely consumed my life. How horrible and revolting, how ugly and frightful was this skirmish. I had run out of words for this loathsome debacle. At the same time I was beside myself with joy and the wretched delirium of my mental state.

'Where are we off to,' I queried. 'Your choice' he said. And I replied with the name of a neighboring town which seemed to excite him. 'Are you headed that far' I sighed, with feigned manners. 'I certainly am,' he responded. After this he began discussing the tomatoes and his good crops that were plentiful in these gentle spring rains. I, at once, felt a mood coming on, anxious to prod him into my corral. That is, unearthing his true motives for the likes of me and I asked him point blank 'what are you up to, today?' In fact I nearly roared and I hastened, don't you know, what prompted him to pick me up. To be sure I was spent shaking my fists at these devils and black-guards. With great reservations I told him, of course, that I had a sneaking suspicion that those around me were up to no good. He merely nodded obviously taken by surprise with my honesty and valor.

It seemed a favorable time to broach the subject of my rivals. Before departing a man at the crossroads at the signal light seemed to bow. Now I was at my wit's end. I would be left to hitch-hike back to the village square. I was nearly used up with this last volley. If I could only venture out as the crow flies I would be as happy as a lark. But no, and these rebels were still up to their mischief. I had, it seemed, been robbed of any emotion or direction to my whereabouts. The throes of my imagination had left only foolish talk and these repugnant episodes lay in the stagnant air for me to traverse. However, to weather this automata, the mechanical behavior and teetering universe, these imps at the fore, was more than I could do.

So down the esplanade I scrambled, thumb out, on the ready for new prospects. Suddenly and without warning a sports car pulled over. I chose to be more forthcoming this time. Yes, I would take the bite out of these musings by pledging my services to these demons at the fore. But all of my trials lay without results. I swore off that I would commit no more hocus pocus at my elbows. Still I must run the gambit of these forbearers.

At home I spent the better part of the night rehearsing my lines and my introduction to these miscreants that had passed my way. How could they so thoroughly dissolve my wishes? They were simply henchman practiced at the art of deception, nothing less, nothing more.

I was of the opinion, of course, that this puppet show must cease. But who was I to ask as much seeing as how everybody and his brother was in denial of this diurnal deceit. Oh, heaven, I scowled, what was to become of me! My tricks, perhaps, had cost me a dear price as had this nervous state that, as I have said before, held me by the collar.

Awakening to the brilliant gloss of day I was in one of my rare moods. I was in the mood of complete forgiveness such as was seen only in the make believe. If those responsible would only come forth, as I begged, I would make full allowances for a reprieve to these horrors. Exonerating the past for the present we would march together no longer riddled by the mischief of these hordes that followed me night and day. But really were my nerves up to it? I was isibly shaken and I trembled inside at the conditions of this truce. Nevertheless, perseverance had seen me through the roughest of times and why should this be any different.

I managed to make one step at a time. I was plenty cautious of this preamble to bury the hatchet altogether though I was prepared to go the extra mile to accommodate these fledglings of the absurd. I must say, my children, that it gives me no rest to see you fornicate with these devils at my side. None, whatsoever!

And so with a few shiny coins I entered the barber shop bent on getting a shave and haircut, to prepare myself for this great turn of fate. Surely I would soon be a successful author and I must, I thought, look the part. The part, that is, of dignity. If all else failed I would procure a job sweeping up at some hole-in-the-wall.

The barber asked if he knew me, presumably from some other walk of life. When I responded, no, he went about his business with a hot towel and clippers, and before I knew it he had clipped my hair and beard without a second thought. Who, I wondered, was he in this vast array of matters. Certainly he had been informed of my treacherous status. Meanwhile an ambulance roared down Fifth Street as I departed pressed and groomed for a holiday.

I wheedled out of a gratuity with good manners and proceeded down the esplanade with my new look. It would seem that those about me were quite taken. After all, I appeared as though I had recently acquired a fresh and striking quality and I wasn't about to invent myself once again. Must I shout that I wouldn't leave you crying, my dear friends. Oh but this crowd has me coming and going. I am no more here than there. Believe me you can beat yourselves with a stick and it will mean nothing to me. Nothing.

II

The days flew past and as no confirmation arose to be published I ventured to town for employment. I had been rescued from hunger and shelter by collecting bottles and cans. But how could I continue this time consuming enterprise. As luck would have it the third restaurant that I visited needed a dishwasher. Whether this was the workings of these scoundrels tailing me I couldn't tell. Nonetheless it was money sorely needed. Though I wasn't fond of it, it was a necessary evil and certainly, I thought, my writing would redeem me from this menial task. And so I enjoyed my post as much as possible and the monies it would bring to send out my manuscript.

Soon, none too soon, while scouring the pots and pans it dawned on me that, perhaps, foul play with my manuscript was preventing me from publication. This irritated me to no end. I was prepared to travel the distance myself to one of the publishing houses if it would prevent their acts of disruption. However, this would cost a pretty penny and therefore would take some time.

Fortunately in two days time from these considerations I finally received a favorable reply to my submission. I was ecstatic! My poor brain wasn't used to such acceptances and I was reeling from their words 'beautifully written' and 'filled with many strengths.' 'Beautifully written' and 'filled with many strengths' I repeated over and over. Well, I said to myself, I was an author and not merely a dishwasher. I decided that it was wise to quit my work

and to donate my time to my true post.

An artist, at last, I proposed.

At such a time I was, it appeared, on my druthers. I had been stripped of any ill-awill and I was dedicated to polishing off a novel in the future. After all, I was a man of the world and I wouldn't permit my nemesis to do me irrevocable harm. If they had it in for me I would only blossom that much more, stubborn as a mule, never cowering in the face of this adversity. I would let them go about their business, no doubt, pulling off the wings of flies.

And, thus, I would let them all know on no uncertain terms the man that I was capable of being without flinching or driving home the nail. Yes, never would they again use me for their ill-begotten schemes. I was gaining ground, gladdened and even delighted and exalted in the swathes of their miserable selves. Must I shout now the claims they proposed against me. Their mandates were only laughable in the face of my literary charms but believe you me I scowled more than once over their trespasses.

I was running quite a fever amidst the acceptance of my submission and, more times than not, I wished that I might meet face to face my rivals in this chase. Still I wouldn't say that it was a great pleasure knowing you. Instead I would give them all a pat on the back and a smirk at their deliveries, biting and untrue. The acid irony of them giving me the boot drew no tears though I was circumspect at finding myself slain if I didn't hold vigil in the face of their indignities.

Their promises, their covenants, if you will allow me, were only mentally exasperating. While there was something mildly crude about their proposals the course and motions of their opposition was deeply despicable and their appeals were entirely without merit. But I wasn't above locking the door despite these oftentimes tame voices coming out of the woodwork. The truth be known I would give my heart gladly to an honest soul. No, I wouldn't hang my head in shame of what was being suggested, those propositions that might be better left unsaid.

But by now the darkness has once again fallen and I have no recourse to other terms. Let us beg and borrow from the fund of thought neither giving up the ghost nor stepping on the toes of those before me.

This morning my whole body convulsed and gave me a start but I was no longer inspired. Sooner or later your grandchildren would be reading me, and no doubt, sobbing I crowed and I most likely would be dead if these last throes were any indication of my health. Indeed, I shook from within my own bony skull. I smarted in my temples but I wouldn't relinquish this suffering for another recourse no matter what pain it cost me. I was still on the right track and this much was undeniable. Still I could no longer look in the mirror. My looks had dissipated into only the shadow of a man.

The wind today has been fierce and my soul hasn't recuperated from this blast of cold. Instead I weep and wonder recalling from memory this toast to all affronts. Where is the loving path to my redemption, I cried. Perhaps a walk in the garden would slow my fatal heart in these foul and obtuse proceedings. My heart and soul, what blandishments await me. I would do well to coax these several others into their own pens. There was no gainsaying it. I was in an uproar to cast away these influences and to come straightaway to a land less inscrutable.

Don't sweat it; I said aloud, what burdens go before us? Who knows, perhaps, they are rising above and beyond their call of duty. Oh, yes, the faces come alive and I am no more a man than yesterday. What restless darlings have I at my disposal? Meanwhile I make tracks on the early train bent on disinterring those before me. I was on the road, it is true, but a more flexible and forgiving man had never come before me! Of this I was certain. I hemmed and I hawed but there were none others that could derail me.

The latest correspondence from the publishing house has revealed that it would be, perhaps, one year until my publication. My dreams were diminished and appeared to be broken with this delay. Indeed, needless to say, I was crestfallen. Apparently there was much work to be done. This I would still pursue to the ends of the earth but it dampened my spirits, to be sure.

The doorbell rang and startled me. Nobody but nobody knew of my presence here and I shook from this interruption. It was an interruption that cut me to the quick seeing as how I was in the midst of editing. In my pajamas I opened the door slightly to get a better look at my visitor. It appeared as though he had the wrong address and soon scurried off presumably to some other residence. Still it was uncertain if he was put up to this inquiry and I loathed his presence in my affairs of annotation.

Soon, judging from the time frame, I would be forced into resuming my job washing dishes. It was paramount to survive. There was no other answer. With some reluctance they hired me back though

I had given them no notice of leaving. So I took to shining the pots and pans as never before writing all the while as I did my duties at the restaurant. Perhaps soon I might assume the job of a waiter, I felt, if my work would so promote me.

Wouldn't you know it soon I was to be a waiter with all the gratuities involved. My allowances would elevate me and whether or not my allies or nemesis made their mark I was still on the run driven by such excesses beyond my control.

It was a Friday. I could remember it well. They had me turning on a dime. But I wasn't lost altogether. I ambled quietly back upstairs to my little hovel and I swallowed my tears. The clouds from the sea came rolling in. There wasn't a divorce so bitter as in these times but I kept the flame going despite the severest of struggles and as I told them 'all' to get fixed I ruminated thus.

Why should a man, any man, come to these terms? I was simply loaded with a manuscript that may not see the light of day? There seemed to be nothing for certain and I scoffed at the possibilities of being refused, retired, and stillborn as an author.

At any rate much work was to be done. The days seemed to have grown longer. While I polished off my editing skills I stood erect much of the time. Still the paranoia that lay by my side was enough to deflect me as I held great promises into the future.

Are my dreams forsaken or not. I needed my trophy and I was adamant about receiving it. Why should I shiver with remorse? The deed was done and the experiments continued without surcease.

The experiments, that is, that engaged me with this struggle. Straight away into the night I could hear the sound waves rattle my cage. Meanwhile I smiled at the games we played at our leisure and I swore to kingdom come that I would never let them take me alive. What gargoyles would they have me bear I said not without a sort of rapture and a tear in my eyes?

I went about my business as never before, striking forth on behalf of the written word. Yes, I was strong and able on the brink of something abounding from some higher power. But after all I wouldn't bow to just anyone. And I laughed to beat hell.

Perhaps there were brighter days to be seen. One couldn't tell what ravages awaited me. This much was certain, as I have said before; I absolutely wouldn't cower nor surrender. I would tear into these others without compromise.

Today the trains were running and I decided upon a visit to other lands, ones that would come to me without effort and which might be a relief from both allies and my nemesis alike. The rains were ushering in and I was jubilant about my new itinerary. At first, that is. The library and a park bench both called my name out in welcome. I swore that never again would I return to that little room that was haunted in such a deep and wandering way. Still the cold seemed to bite into me and I felt ashamed at being homeless. I turned abruptly on Buffingdom way and crossed to Euclid Avenue. I wasn't out of the woods yet until I reached Laurel Avenue which housed the library. There I would remain safe from the onslaughts of the weather as well as safe from the clutches of the world. Ever since I was young I had been a patron of the library and the Y.M.C.A. It was no different today. Today I was, as then, riddled with bare necessities. I would suppose that I had always been driven by the hard road. It seemed to be my nature. I longed for love as before, an unrequited love. But merely to wish doesn't make it true. Such thoughts occupied me making me nervous about my future. Over land and sea I had traveled and where was I to take my place among you. I begged of you to take me under your wings, but for what? The morning comes and the garden is spread out. My obsessions are stealing away into the night. I am a blind man in so many ways.

Once upon a time through my lover's kind words I captured my soul late in the night. The dusty road was behind me and, mercy me, I would sing you a song upon so many miles that I had miraculously traversed. I had the weather upon my brow. Meanwhile I yawned. The strangers were nothing but a bother. I strove for words that would make me more than misty, those that would reach into my gut.

And there I sang the troubadour of the times.

I walked on and on and I had become quite the chatterbox in my exploits. A part of me wished only to give up while the other was adamant about staying alive no matter what the price. Yes, the minstrel I was, steeped in melancholy. I assumed a form of madness that lay elsewhere. All of possession engulfed me. I stood straight up and began to write. Oddly enough it didn't matter what I wrote only that I wrote. This was paramount!

So I broke my heart as I leaned toward the rooftops, swearing off any more cursives of this wandering. All solace had forsaken me. I was no closer to gaining ground than before and my stance, if you could call it that, was to paw at the eternities that lay before me. In the meantime the ambulance drove by me. I was, indeed, stuck in its maw. If my heart should cease to matter I would still cry out to the scores of others so that I might forfeit my post. What if I cried out loud? What if I proposed that it didn't matter? Oh, well, I shall spit and weave these themes. Hmm! I sighed. I wished that sentimentality played no part, nevertheless, it did. Mine seemed to be to brood among these ruins and to heed the restlessness and horror of it all.

So up I crawled to my little room from the past, unannounced. There lay the disorder of the linens that I had left. Upon the stoop I sat absolutely drunk about these wanderings. There I paused sweating buckets in this clime, dizzy with emotion. What would I contrive, what would I conspire to release these dormant others, flailing their arms and making mischief. I tell you, it is no good! My life has come to a standstill. I merely always wanted to go home! Ah, but to go home!

III

Once upon a time the tableau of sea and sky was breached and there was nothing more to do then to grapple with and restore one's senses. The strength and nature of my nemesis was indeterminate. However, in this small town, I hung mad with rage. The homes flapped in the respiration of the bright bunting, the placards, and the gonfalons streaming along the city walls. I prowled, side by side, in the shroud of light with the fantastic bloom of flowers. But each footstep was at odds with the rivers of darkness that began to pour over me. Only a weak rain gave me solace as sweet as kisses, and touched the sky, sometimes mottled with light.

Nonetheless, oh! How I loved life and visited it in between the embattled
39
discourse with these damned sirens as much as possible. Yes, the substance mixed with the phantoms and phantasms had me reeling with worry.

What were the concessions to be made? Why would my enemy almost never reply to my questions directly? What was there object? Why so sinister unless it be toward my end. That was it! That must be it! The hash marks of the beginning dictated it. The heartaches, the thunderous cries and constant yammering to change my conduct, to still my rage, and control my revolt, and prevent this wild, free-fall at their bidding.

Oh, my heart be still. Such a

superhuman and horrible fury indistinguishable, now and then, from the chattering heavens. Even the dreadful calm, do you understand, was filled with feeble and haunting utterances, and there was nowhere to go. Nowhere!

The waves clambering against the wind, the warped pilings and the soft mittens of the sand, a few wispy clouds, and the golden sun striking the sea like a gong. And later a luminous stone, the moon beckoning to love. Ah! When the moon was never so quiet and laid its soft flame upon the earth. When the sun blazed its trail upon the long, cool rivers and struck the mountain tops, I clutched at the fundament of its silent wisdom and I wandered the valley of voices, and there I wailed before the height of the sky, and registered each reply with shock.

Daily did I walk and witness a path of

the sea rowing with great oars to shore, the brine in the solemn air, the breath of each wave, the floating of the kelp beds swaying like headdress. My exordium upon that one infamous day. If one could be named. At home the mellow sunlight in the kitchen, as from an ancient torch, and the curtains drawing breath like a bellows. What's more the hollow feeling inside as I inhaled the shadows? And me a victim of nothing demonstrable. Or the endless gibberish, cluttering my mind, as I hobbled like a tramp by the train tracks.

Upon this night there was no way that I could return to my haunted room,

especially with the nervous vigor that coursed through my veins. I was falling into bad times it would seem and I chose to spend the money I earned from being a waiter for the sanctity of fresh lodging. Though I could easily guess that

45

malevolence would follow me my only sensible recourse was to at least try to free myself from the chains girding my forsaken mind. I found an inexpensive dwelling. It smelled of curry and I was handled with cursory haste.

Obviously they knew exactly who I was. I left my door opened to reveal my knowledge of the vigilance all about me. No more than one hour passed when I could no longer play this passive part. I stood at the threshold and I screamed 'cowards, cowards' into the night air. Well, not a soul stirred even though I was shrieking at the top of my lungs. Weeping and hiccupping I pursued these demons with resolute fury. However, after a spell of this lively occasion I decided to hit the road and distance myself from this foxhunt. Everywhere people came and went as tightly as a wound clock! To this swinging pendulum all I witnessed in other's eyes was mortal terror. And in their eyes there was bred no need to abdicate. The strength of a species. To make this chase worthy of my brains and brawn, this undying struggle, made me both stronger and more agile. Oh! Find me a wishing well that accepts forlorn dreams, my dear fool. Not the most enviable position, but I must write for the beloved children and wife I would never know.

All voices of this devil have been silenced. Hurrah! I cry out with each passing day for these idle moments. To what I owe this to is arcane, occult, and secretive. I often sit with tenderness, thinking of more gentle and playful times. My eyes are moist with tears, my humor is growing. I find that my neighbor is schizophrenic and is affected by his symptoms. There is nothing that I can do. Occasionally, I will hear him talking to himself, cursing and denouncing his voices. This will give rise to my past indiscretions, to the ignes fatui with which I was formerly plagued, with which I was crushed. But presently my spirits have picked up.

The other day I passed by a mirror and, again, I failed to recognize myself. In due time now I have deserted my post as a waiter. I don't mind that I am being groomed for an idiot's job, shelving books. One of my strengths has been adaptability and chameleon that I am; I should get along quite handsomely. Perhaps eventually I will try my luck abroad. Nevertheless, matters seemed to insist that I should stay put. And so I shall!

Among the enormous shelves of books in the quiet I will sometimes stop to examine a few passages. At least nobody here will get on my back nor abuse me with criticism. Here it is cool and I feel like I am coming into my own. The staff seems reasonable and the patches of light through the big bay windows are very pleasing. It is only part time and it doesn't try my patience. Quite the contrary, these books were once alive and my dear friends.

The memory of my misfortunes is beginning to disappear. This morning I arose naked, singing a familiar tune. Things were certainly picking up. It was my day off and I promised myself to make a visit to the sea. Over hill and dale I took a bus past a small lake and through winding roads of trees and big ranches. Soon I was running along the coast by the side of the chutes and ladders of the waves. My appetite for these waters was immeasurable. The cool depths seemed to caress me as I sprayed water into the blue sky. After sunning myself upon the beach my blood began to throb in my temples and I reluctantly decided to head for home.

For now no longer is there the horrid and revolting presence of the damned sirens. No longer is there the divorce from genuine life nor the horror, the absolute horror of IT! The only bedtime sounds are the sweet sounds of the summer crickets. A mild breeze might awaken the mellifluous chimes on the porch or brush the vines on the trellis. However, there are no more disturbances than these and I count my blessings for this sanctuary, cradled in bed. Yes, there are no more promising covenants than believing in oneself and the rare but fruitful correspondences with my friends and family help to give me back my identity, my name. I have come this far to finally visit my old cronies, a married couple who show their warmth and politeness and compassion at any metamorphosis that I might declare.

Nothing was said to betray their love. In the great northwest we laughed by the sea like old times and I found it fairly easy to hide from any hallucinogenic state. If such a thing presented itself. For certain I was a man returning from the dead. My voracious appetite for life was emerging. Quite clearly there were good times to be had. Mine was to enjoy every minute.

My resplendent and tender friends could see that I was in a little state of disrepair and gave to me a few shirts, a jacket, a hat, and a pair of pants. I felt ashamed for letting myself go to the dogs as such but their generosity was entirely without recriminations. Soon I would leave and my lonely self would reappear.

On the train I began to write once again. But wait! I can hear the neighbors singing in the next club car. Is it a band of gypsies? I chortled to myself. They have lovely voices and their song is filled with promise. At least there is always solace to be found somewhere.

Summer's hot and honey breath, the long shadows of autumn would soon appear. But for now the high blue heavens and the slender sea is exhausted at the tide. I must bare and beat my chest. Angels in the dark, peering through my eyes, youthful exuberance, the sadness of it all, the sadness! The trails of light and shadow, autumn's mist, autumn's brume is to come. Should I paint a watercolor of Venice or Corfu? My deepest fear that I may not be anybody, though I rant and rave.

You pound and you pound! Why are you cross with me? Shadows beg and borrow. My invincible song, the wind snagged in the bellows, the roses snipped =back, in and out to the trampling sea. I beg forgiveness from day to night for my importunities. Oh twilight, when the

ghosts no longer march to the triumphant
wave and call of the little, pale sirens, I
retire without compromise to the
garden of polished stones and the kindled
stars. I will, henceforth, sit beside you to
notarize my true signature in the soft,
promising wind. And now it is five

o'clock in the morning. The coffee has
percolated and the thin air is still chilled. I
gather my thoughts by the wayside, the

mixed and the matched, and gently move

toward the sea. My mind is unhinged and
races with the sprinting waters along the
mellow dunes where burly waves patiently
dissolve into fingers that slowly clasp the
entire shore. If you listen, if you give it
all up, you can hear the ancient's galleys
rattle their chains beyond the horizon. One
thing is for certain, I would never write a
real book. Why spin a yarn? After all,
there are greater successes than art. Just

to live is enough!

IV

It was a sleepless night. One might say, the night before last, as fresh as it remains in my mind. It was clearly a matter of nerves. I was rudely reminded of when madness had approached me. It was as though the earth had rolled from off its axis. It was a day that even love couldn't entirely heal. To this day I shudder to think of it. Yes, bathing in this infernal gloss of the

light and its excessive warmth was my fate, a fate which I have sworn off with all my limited powers. I remain impassive from my dose of psychotropic medicine and in the hot sun I shamble to and fro. By now I realize, in hindsight, that these drugs are, for the most part, mere placebos. The heat was vexing but really nothing more. It was predictable. No? I must learn, once again, how to see! In my writing I would like to move benignly from thought to thought with purpose; but, alas, it is not my manner. It would constitute a story of which I am now incapable. It is disappointing but I can no longer play the part of the hero. Still, to risk an absurdity, there is an heroic form of paranoia, like a form of astuteness, that seems to be a permanent fixture. The dye is cast and there is no retreating. Perhaps it is a vestige of good will. Come join me, eh, and thence we will howl at the moon. It does me no good to reproach me for my honesty. Believe you me it would take a fecund imagination to manage the portrait of my anxiety. In this regard I promised myself to redouble my efforts, for my efforts were effete. Such an awakening had me down but I wouldn't permit this caprice to do me in. If I was to do wrong so vehemently in my portrait wouldn't I suffer from remorse and wouldn't this contrition poison me?

But surely, as things stand, this is the nightmare of somebody else. I ask the powers of this world to negotiate a time soon when 'they' would be coming for me. It is true. I am a runabout in modern life. In this harsh light compromises, I realize, must be made. However, I suffer from the oppression one feels when his back is against the wall. The judgments imparted against me are cruel, and there is no escape. Oh, but I have come far from the beginning when my nemesis shouted out proclamations for all to hear, like the town crier. I wouldn't be astonished if 'they' had an exhaustive dossier about me from birth to the present. With utter and surprising calm I have submitted myself to this unthinkable element knowing, no longer, where to tread. But for now I was knee deep in hoopla and I wouldn't ruin the day steeping myself in my own troubles or the woes of others. Yes, today there was no need to frown and I would yield in the face of any danger rather than pursuing it as before. I would take a wonderful respite from discerning these masks surrounding me. Perhaps I would take another trip to the environs that paled to the denseness of the city. I would relish the terms of my mettle, singing to my brethren, without fishing for clues to my imprisonment. Sitting on a bench I was privy to remembrances of my youth. I began to recall my first romantic tryst. I was fortunate enough to have a good teacher who excelled in the tantric art of embrace. It would seem that from the beginning, almost without exception, the women that I dated had a history of infidelity. So much so that as time passed I couldn't believe in any of them. This original teacher was a salesgirl. Innocent enough and yet she was gifted in these sensuous writings. I was, from the outset, sympathetic toward her. I asked her to join me in coffee and she assented. In the conclusion to our date I awkwardly pressed her hand with my own and I bade her goodbye. I found lust was manifest in her smile and I promised to myself that I would return. In bed I experienced her peremptory manner alternating with the obsequious manners of a maid. At the same time in public I discovered that she had wandering eyes. I could see into the future, our future, when she wouldn't give me the time of day. Her promiscuity weighed heavily upon me. In contrast to her, a year or so later I met my first and only wife. She saved me from a life of debauchery. Her great humor endeared me to her. The other day I came upon an album of photographs that were, perhaps, responsible in part, for my present frame of mind. It contained, among other things, a portrait of her before we were separated by her death in an automobile accident. It appeared so fresh in memory that I couldn't register her disappearance from my life.

With both thankfulness and ingratitude I clutched at these memories with tears in my eyes and I faintly smiled.

I awoke, smoked a cigarette in bed, and ventured out the door to a café close by. There nobody said a word. Everyone was busy with the newspaper or their computer. As though I was controlled by other forces I poured myself a black coffee and I moved to take a chair. I stared at a painting on the wall for sale. It was exorbitant in price and it nettled me thinking of my efforts to get published. For some reason I was reminded of the circus and I became anxious to leave. Perhaps I was thinking that I was playing the part of the clown. However, soon I shrank from this intuition hastening home to do my laundry.

I had my radio on but I couldn't hear it from the din of the street below my balcony. Tomorrow would be a holiday, I was thinking. Then there was a knock at the door. It was the custodian of the building checking on the working order of the smoke detectors. I carried on with conversation but with disinterest and soon he left. I ate standing up at the balcony but there was a couple across the street that appeared to be arguing as they were both gesticulating wildly. But as it was none of my business I closed the door and went about my own affairs. Nevertheless there seemed to be a brawl forming down the hallway as well and I began to wonder if these were both acts of conspiracy against my peace of mind. As I couldn't name their content explicitly I drifted off to other thoughts. Later I heard a thud from the upstairs apartment and this was my last observation before I fell asleep.

In the morning I stuck my head out the bedroom window and I stared at the green hillsides. It was now a holiday and as I heard no noise from the street I closed the window on the cold outside. The quiet reminded me of Sunday though it was Thursday and I was a little put off. I was a creature of habit, as they say, and I didn't like things that were out of this ordinary flow that constituted my happiness. It struck me that, like it or not, I was in a different world today. And so I turned to writing things of familiarity, entertaining myself with anecdotes of my youth. Yet it seemed to me that I was troubled from the outset though I hadn't realized it at the time. But I pushed on to the hilt, weighing the importance of these revelations, until a shrill whistle from the teapot awoke me from this strain. It was a day to stoke a fire place if I had one but I had to settle upon a heavy coat as the heater wasn't working either. In my emptiness I began to wonder if there was something in the world to emulate but I came to the conclusion that there wasn't and that old age was 'round the corner. Still it wasn't that disagreeable and I began to enumerate objects in the room divisible by fifteen. At times I would amuse myself with this practice for hours at a time. My condition, after all, wasn't any more severe than the next fellow and it was a far cry from the human misery that I witnessed at the hospital in which I had once worked. Yes, it certainly wasn't as elegiac as those terms from what seemed like ages ago and I doubled over crying out and strenuously objecting to these perceptions of far away until they lost their vigor. And I began to laugh with abandon for the first time in a great while as if I was in the throes of death and it didn't matter. Every thought and everything became ridiculous now as did my so-called sickness and I laughed to beat hell disowning any debt to my foolish rages of the past. It finally dawned upon my tired brain that it would be wise to submit a letter, cautiously worded, to the local newspaper. Therein I would take the initiative to set things right with my foes and allies alike. They would surely see that, though I wasn't a flawless moralist, I was, nevertheless, not a wicked person by any means. Who, after all, deserved this shameful infamy and abusive acrimony that had induced me to take the awkward steps that I had traveled thus far. There was no more damning testimony to my feeble life. I had been reduced to a travesty, clinging to every fledgling by my shoulder, and I was disconsolate no matter what triumph I had drawn in face of this despondency. My chief complaints against this netherworld were owned, as well, by my cohorts, far and near, and were too numerous to mention. Meanwhile I was no more than a platitude despite my efforts. We were aliens together, without solace. Still, without sorrow, I have maintained my position. Though I would have liked to have been more elegant in my delivery I could, nevertheless, brag about some of the entries to my diary. But now it is time to splash some water on my face and begin my letter.

To Whom It May Concern:

Althought there are those among you that would quip about these words and could attach a face to them I am not sorcerer enough, do you hear me? I am not sorcerer enough to create an abyss in which I would so easily fall. Nor do I have the imagination necessary to expound in great length the record of my travels both mental and physical which has led me by my collar to this day of profound troubles. I can see you now doubling over with irrepressible laughter, asking expressly, these shadows what do they know? For is it with misunderstanding that I pounce upon you and your so-called ccompassion and clemency? You must see for yourselves that I come and go, sometimes without shelter and food, and that if I hadn't been so dreadfully timid I might have exerted myself and my efforts as I deemed fit. Oh, but I can hear the striking of a gavel now as if I was accosted by the court. In my behavior I am defensive by the nature of the accusations made against me, made no doubt to disinter me of the noble birth, as a man of some distinction worth more than your febile insults. After all is said and done about my trials I, nevertheless, have enough personality to deploy to save me from your imcomprehensive banter. For example the other day, at the library, I was introduced to a subject with some rudeness and these poor manners were put upon me in such a way as to force my hand.

In this same vein I must ask you to explain yourself as I wasn't guilty of any crime, great or small. Please reply to my post office box and, indeed, take no offense at these observations made in an amicable light. The shadows with which I am plagued will take care of themselves in due time. After all, I have no twin in these matters and if I was to I would address them post haste. I don't wish to burden you with the excessiveness of this crime nor to suggest that there are others among us capable of this sorcery. Forgive me for the desultory nature of these remarks as I am a little under the weather today. Anyway, don't bother ruffling your feathers with these words of mine meant for the sake of understanding and good faith.

Ever thine,
R.C.

By now I was dressed in rags. My pants were quite loose as I had been forced to diet with my infrequent meals. I was no longer the lubber as before these hardships arrived. But for now life's corruptions were filled with insults and tenuous vapors that stalked me day and night. All my attention was focused on stonewalling these imps and devils at my side or behind me. I began to tick off my list of subjects to explore in writing. In this way I might avoid the obstructions that I faced in the anarchy of my mind. But what awaited me? Was I searching, now, for an asylum but without others woes? How was I to undo what I had so foolishly done?

Though my body was again, plain and simple, my memory wasn't at all wizedend. I discovered that it was most remarkable that things should come to this and I vowed to take these foreign elements without restraint others woes? How was I to undo what I had so foolishly done?

Though my body was aging, plain and simple, my memory wasn't at all wizened. I discovered that it was most remarkable that things should come to this and I vowed to take these foreign elements without restraint. Nevertheless, today the sky was breached by the sun and in this immortal groove it stabbed at me with abandon. Moreover it fell into the bottomless sea where dark promises breed far from the little splashes of water at my feet sucking the pebbles smooth. I wandered the beach like a wingless Icarus awaiting the cool breezes of evening and I nursed myself on visions of the future. Where the sky was rent this light pelted down mercilessly upon the shore and I sat myself down upon the bulwarks of the seawall. Momentarily I was disturbed and I found myself prowling to and fro, once again, my patience running thin. My skin was burning from the fire in the sky and my breathing was stifled. I felt, at once, drowsy and a little muzzy from the gusts of heat drumming up from the sand, bleeding me like a leech. But for now all that I could do was to shelter myself in the shade where some picnic benches and trees lay with a small refreshment stand. I longed for a thirst quencher to invigorate me but, of course, I was without any money. I noticed that, in the portable rooms nearby, the swimmers changed in and out of their street clothes and it was occupied by people that would simply vanish behind closed doors never to be seen again. Yes, by some token they thence ceased to be. It was more than a little unnerving and I chose to wend on before something evil attacked me. And so I happened upon the laundry mat where I could sit in the cool air. I took out my pencil and pocket notebook to make some simple observations. I licked the tip of my pencil and I wandered through the territory of my new book.

Were these uncharted waters, black magic, witchcraft, or a form of collusion to rub me the wrong way? What, on earth, was happening with these tropes and figures of speech? What, on earth, was I doing? Was there no escape from these exasperating pranks of the underworld? They were, without a doubt, sinister and were not without presentiments. Despite my difficulties 'they' were making of me a hero once again. For the sake of appearance I leapt up trying my luck at other avenues while my murmurings fell upon me. Shuttling forth I looked over my shoulder to espy only an ocean seeming as empty as a grave. I was feeling corrupted and I deeply shook from these intuitions at my elbows. I pursued other newborn machinations upon the horizon. I would need a dexterous conversant to interpret the monologue of my enemies and add to this I was at my last straw. Mine was, at last, to take the initiative to rescue myself from absent minded expressions. One could easily see the blankness of my visage and the stammering manner that I couldn't shake. But this noise about me was mere obstreperousness designed, perhaps, to induce me to sing my praises unashamedly amongst my so-called colleagues. And make no mistake they were as querulous today as ever and depraved as well. In the meantime I lay as stupid as a stick fending them off their sloping course with only a sick smile. To the patrons and pedestrians that I would pass I was no more than a travesty with which to avoid and today, again, I was miserable from their chatter. Under a cloud I hobbled muttering to my accusers of their crimes and shouting out with remonstrance. Soon enough I would caper from their gab, if I was fortunate enough and I would find myself wading in patience. Even while my suspicions and duplicity grew I was only a jack of all trades and a master of none. My only respite was to obtain that which was in my field of vision and to domesticate the interlocutors within.

In the distance you could hear the crack of thunder. It was a rare occurrence and I welcomed it without a hitch though it was incongruous with my unruly voices. All in all the landscape, what with its thunder and lightening, was felicitous to my senses. Yes, it inspired beauty together with primitive instincts. As I was out in the open I ventured with celerity to a tree for shelter from the torrid rain. At this I suffered from a little apprehension. But for the sky lit up by lightening the distance was swarthy. The fellows and ladies at my back seemed to be excited in these climes. Time was precious to not only me, but to them as well. In the last analysis they seemed to me a little peculiar but then caprice was their rite of passage. Fancy that! Of all the hallmarks one could venture it was with utter disdain that they should be guilty of this scar which blemished them. With all of their impulses and flings where was I to go? Should I lay down for the imperfect science of psychoanalysis? But why should I take it upon myself to disabuse them systematically of their sophistry? In the distance I could see the window of my little room and I was reminded of the visit I had from a neighbor last night. Graceful enough she approached me begging, at last, to be forgiven but that she needed a little money, anything I could spare, for her supper. In retrospect, I must confess, it was thoughtless of me to turn her out. Besides there was a note of compassion in her manner. She had a faint mustache as some women do and I noticed that she had the habit of saying 'ludicrous' even when it wasn't the correct word or necessarily added to her meaning. Who knows, perhaps, it might have been a budding kinship of which I was, at the time, unaware. But the anomalies of that night were many as if everyone knew that I was an easy touch, a target good for the taking. I couldn't very well hide from their intrusions and mischievous patter. And so I told them, straightaway, that they would have to try other outlets and I left it at that. I suppose that I did this selfishly with a blind eye toward their needs. Was it a possibility that my luck would not turn my way if these were merely crucibles with which providence was testing me? I wasn't, after all, a devout patron of the pantheon of these menacing voices at my backside. Still who could accuse me of selfishness toward my fellow man after all that I had given and endured.

There was absolutely no venom nor hatred toward these compatriots at my side. Moreover, I had conducted myself with honor, nobility, and respect toward all of these strangers and distant friends alike. It had been summers ago since I had first encountered these troubles of today. Just to think of all the water under the bridge made my body rush. But it was morning now and I was out in the street. Without notice a young fellow, like an urchin, knocked off my beret. I looked at him with disgust and slightly afraid of things coming to blows.

Nonetheless, he kept marching with an insolent smirk on his face, almost capering with delight. After a while, thinking it all over in the cool of time, I began to resent my actions, or my lack of them, and my obvious cowardice in face of this showdown. This confrontation presently intrigued me to no end. To clutch at his overcoat and show him the back of my hand seemed the action to take. I would return him back his scorn with a flout of my own and dexterous with my words insult him to no end. Dreaming thus I would seal his inexorable fate with my own two hands. He could very well defame me but I would not surrender. I would answer him back with a gravelly voice. Perhaps if my friends were to show themselves we might bivouac beneath the symmetry of the spheres awaiting this rude gentleman to show himself and to take some of his own medicine. The consternation he had dealt to me in the beginning and his crookedness would be his downfall. About this I would expound to my heart's content. I would show no delicacy in these matters and I would cut a caper of my own to match his original offense. No, he wouldn't have the ghost of a chance with which to reply. It might be a very good opportunity for my allies to vouch for me; as the powers that be know that I am dearly owed. But as time passed I simmered down and, in fact, surprised myself forgetting the incident altogether.

Sauntering about town, milling about here and there, I came upon a church and decided to take a rest at its steps. I was feeling a rich sense of the sacred and of beauty but otherwise I was entirely without piety. No, I wouldn't abase myself before any other or any doctrine. With such acute discernment I would adopt the corporeal wherein the senses would awaken the tangible. Mine wasn't to disembody myself with madness. I would take the easy road and soar with infallibly good taste. Smitten as such I took my leisure climbing the spires to peer at every aspect of the valley below. From this indissoluble height I would let go of my immutable delirium, calling upon each and every crook of the road no matter what the outcome. Though 'they' might hang me in effigy I would continue at my post without faltering. Toward this fabled end I would derive respect deserved me and I would confound them all, my friends and nemesis as well. I would not let them rob me of the ineffable madness of which I was still subject from time to time. After all I was still seized with an able bodied volition with which to spar with these demons. One could say that I was sadly infested with the maxims of the insane. No matter how hard I try I am still not abstemious enough to make mundane sense with my moods and words and, moreover, I am incapable of managing an even keel. Oh, but what grandeur is there to descry the distant and obscure if, with these mutterings, one is no closer to the truth or clarity of any kind. My incompetence weighs heavily upon me as does my indolence and languor. Contrary to public thought I still suffer from concussions of the sacred and profane though I am inept at naming them. Surely enough I will have my next repast to enjoy. Oh, well, mum's the word I say, with great jest, and "the devil fetch the hindmost."

V

The town was deserted and I felt utterly alone. Even the marketplace was barren and nowhere, as before, did any merchant present himself to haggle over prices of the items. I found myself in complete isolation upon this holiday. But for the life of me with no amount of struggle could I quit these surges of speech so curious at my backside. Oh, but do they ever bruit about with such disguised gossip and innuendo.

At times I would rush forth incognito, with an ace bandage wrapped around my head, riveted in my new identity, my new pose. Nonetheless, it was an impossible setting filled with my own groans and remonstrance. Still I was aghast. Why not a soul stirred and I wasn't any longer going to have any of those resembling me in the least come forth on their terms and not my own. With this disguise I protested but without bitterness. But no amount of struggle seemed to see me through this indignation and I was, indeed, left to humorous devices to rescue me from their skittish peril. I ambled to and fro until I reached the watery earth, the principle of Thales, the amnion of Moby Dick, and I sat down in the spangled light, in the profundities of this chase.

Later, of leaden waters beneath leaden skies I shed a tear until time, place, and monomania consumed me. And there I obtained my desolation in the eyeless course of my own misery. And there without a host to my speechless anger did I abide among these nameless ruins without the feline throngs of yesterday. The sea lay vast and undying and the lowering sky advanced to invest the city with its own fog.

It appeared as though bedtime was near and, as I never went out at night, I was prompted to return home. What sanctioned that if not the impenetrable darkness itself and, to boot, it was inseparable from the morbid cold that I endured without a jacket.

Meanwhile, taking to the empty streets, my miscreants were not at all faint-hearted and their aberrations continued without surcease. Again I asked myself without reply was there any shrewd sense to these devils that always wade in the shadows of my footsteps. However, it was more than I could ascertain. I was frustrated with this habitual conception, one without a game plan. I would have to return home with hunger and no food again, or so it seemed until my eyes settled upon a group at the park barbecuing. Inching closer I met up with a gentleman handing out fliers to this gala event celebrating Jesus. Mine wasn't to brood about this off-handed solicitation for I was hungry and their invitation included me despite my head bandage. Perhaps they had been put up to it by some spurious means but really there was no harm in it. If they wished to poison me I would gladly succumb. As it turned out it was a Christian party with an abundance of food and drink. It was only a matter of acting submissive to their overtures and one had a free meal. Of course it was necessary to act the part of the interested novice.

The introductory words of this gentleman made me feel my solitude that much more. In fact it was so complete that I worried about madness enveloping me and I found myself stuffing my face so that I might vanish from this proselytizing shadow. He finally asked me about my bandage and I replied "I limp with my brain, and not my legs." At this he only smiled. I thanked him effusively and told him, simply, that I would consider his remarks and I promptly departed. My belly felt full for the first time in a long while and with this latest form of imprisonment at an end I sauntered toward home whistling at my retreat and congratulating myself on a very fine and patient performance. Well, I had my stroke of good fortune and I didn't allow this perpetrator of fraud, religion, and oblivion put his nose in my affairs. What impostors are among us, my dear friends! Why should I let others betray me with their words? What movements would enhance my position? What working hypothesis should I assume to deal with the arguments I held against these diabolical others? For the life of me I couldn't produce a basis for further theory regarding these matters, so vast and omnipresent.

Like grim death, beneath the shadows of these mutterings, I couldn't forget my monomania and its elusive significance. Moreover, their presence was oftentimes emphatic and fierce and I snatched at anything flexible toward my cause. It was true a part of me was infatuated with the audacious decorum of these idiots and blockheads. However, what was more, heaven knows, was my ineffable solitude and the fact that I couldn't affect nor throw off their shackles. These absurd and ridiculous underlings would tend to overshadow me like the prince of darkness. I tell you every one of their foul intimations only played havoc with my poor soul. Strangely enough I began to wonder if I could live without them. They had been by my side now for a number of summers, scores of them to be exact. Could I not bring to bear the expansive feelings that overwhelmed me at times, my loneliness together with my grandiose ambitions? At times I would fawn over their courtship like an anxious groom. Yes, at times I must say, I loved them to distraction! But, in this connection, I must ask were my best days behind me? If memory serves me well, in their fickleness, I was sometimes forewarned that they bite like a dog. To be so bold I was in good company almost as often as not. Vigilance was my watershed! And if I found myself in a fix I could very well, with good measure, embark upon other terrains.

At home I lay belly down. At the opened window came a fitful blast of wind. With a muffled and plaintive sound came the intrusive voices at my shoulder. I responded sonorously, in studied speech. If my mind was suffering such an eclipse wasn't it up to me to bid them to announce themselves more clearly? Such preoccupations annoyed me but I must, I thought, polish my credentials, so to speak, and preserve my illustrations for the sake of posterity. Such seasonable certainties were at the behest of my sisters and brothers of the public who, at times, reconciled me when I was out of sorts. Toward my infirm and feeble efforts I would have to yield to the time when my spirits were in fine feather. Other than these abstractions, well, I wasn't one whit the wiser. To my knowledge, in my awkward disposition, there was no convention with which to act. I would rise or fall, reckless or not. Was it in my interest to insult these blackguards; to entomb them with my own pert speech? After all they had mocked me time and again while I scattered from their inventions, my insides heaving from their verbal blows. Why should I be inhibited by their insolence, or even their mischief, for that matter? Both were yokes by any name and servitude was not my master. But even with unspeakable fury my cry could not pierce their armor. The prophecies of doom that went before were now upon me. Indispensable proof, perhaps, that all and sundry knew me better than I could imagine. Toward this, with some insistence, I contort my body in its wish to escape. But again, to no avail. It would seem their grip was firm as predators and myself their wounded prey wherever I turned. Such terrible emptiness visited me frequently and, as I have often said, I worried about the fangs of madness digging into me with ultimate vengeance.

VI

I wanted to close my eyes, to lower the
camber of my brow, to sleep forever. No
longer did I want to lisp and stammer at the
supernatural nor permit this jinni to ride
me. My legs tremble as I jettison these
voices. The bile in my sluggish blood
responsible for one or more of the four
cardinal humors. One of my only
certainties, the periodic bereavement of my
soul. These vicious sirens, (if you will),
enter my brain uninvited as through a
needle and syringe. How could life be so
unkind as to one day excise my identity and
seize the workings of my mind?

My adversaries wish to convict me of
a crime. One that I did not commit. What
of language that washes away, efficacy that

forages for some elopement, a silent tongue beckoning for a conclusion. In beauty, not history, I trundle. None shall deny me the happy twittering manner that pours out thanks to my imagination, buttressed with resolution and blanched with sweet nonsense.

Oh, the style of a want to be! I sever this vein of a singularly lonesome fare. But I shall never play into another's hands so easily. No, never! Obstinacy is my engine, is my rudder and sail. My threshold will never be easily traversed. But for now remembrance of my beloved. A few dear images of her flit passed my mind. Her quizzical brow, her beaten copy of Baudelaire, and her etching of a syllabary for the insane into the old boards of a bench. Nearby lies a garden of mint and sweet water. If I were to interpret this now it might read: here lies my true love, thrashed by the heavens, deserted by the earth, and tossed by the forgiving sea.

How to rough out these modern times where I tread cross and wounded by solitude. It appears en masse that I am discounted in every and all conversation, public and private, not knowing which direction to face, whereof to speak, or to move in this colossal, intemperate play. The walls are prompted to speak so lonely am I.

Haggard and pale with exhaustion I, again, weep for mankind. Timidly, but fondly, I gently touch the corolla of a flower wishing myself away from all eyes, all noise, all of the machinery and technology of man. At this rate it is only a matter of time before I am crushed. I am out of humor but although I am not jocular in disposition I am willing to uphold a few simple promises of survival. Yes I believe my turn would come to sit upon the mountaintop.

Perhaps, there, I would be able to steep myself in the features of my trysts, drinking from their throats the libations of love. Thank the lord the firmament was holding steady.

In my ineluctable fate I preened their locks and rearranged their masks. I wooed them with no terminus in mind. Perhaps one day I might be whisked away, scuttling in the vast lanes of the sea to foreign lands. But for now I sat motionless at the park and beneath the vaulted sky I counted the trees that surrounded me. It was true. I was a man, a helpless man, no longer one of professional or moral obligations. No less absurd, I found the grotesque and shrouded sham of these daily proceedings without any merit.

Time and again I threw up my arms, disappointed at the limited radius of my wanderings. Sometimes I would roam the meadows and thickets that lay as sweet as hay. There I witnessed, more than once, the maceration of my will. There I witnessed a world of secrets laid bare before me as I looked incredulous with doubts of my composure. Here I felt madness reaching for me. I began to wonder. Could one go out of his mind without warning signs, without any admonishment whatsoever? Daydreaming thus, after my nap, the spectral evening was so like a flower. From the coffee table I picked up and reread the response of a publication house. Though they hadn't asked for the remainder of my manuscript they, nevertheless, crowned my work with a word of benignancy. This breadcrumb proved to promote my creative ambitions and I made a dash for my pen and paper.

I departed reveling in the cool woods, musing collectively with the stars. I suddenly felt stout with good health and as earlier I dealt my cards decisively. I would imagine that my spirits were soaring due to the infectious mood of sound sleep. One could not emphasize enough the ruins of insomnia.

On the corniche by the sea I often reflected upon my curse, my plague, counseling myself against a death defying leap. Occasionally, I rejoiced even though my head was throbbing from their ministrations. If it was not for mypoltroonery I would have done myself in long ago. I tottered at the brink, perpetually driven by recurring themes, and I finally came to occupy a berth at the rear of a little house. Being a man of scant means this was a perfect dwelling for the time being.

In the distance the church bells rang like crystal. As if I had taken a blow I awoke from a certain vagueness. Reality was fussing to show discernible results. Hunger followed and, as my cupboards were bare, I trekked to town with a caravan on my tail. As most men I had my 'yesses and noes.' To vanish before all others was an unthinkable conclusion. To summon one thus, piteous and blind, I crossed the threshold of deceit. And now I wished for nothing so much as dousing myself with an ampulla of wine.

I was conceived and forty years later I had my fall. I was the subject of one thousand contretemps. However, with nothing left to suppress I was greeted by a branch full of angels. My sense of the sacred would prove to be inviolable. Correspondence with friends was tinctured with hope as the sky was tinctured with blue. Meanwhile my brain was dazzled by the harsh light sitting snugly in its cranial vault. And here my own legends, my memories of innocent joy, emerged. My eyes grew moist as I consulted my past. But the present, at least, was a jubilant day and tonight the pitch arrives except for a few fulgurating stars.

Not an eye in a forest of people has grazed my presence. The delicacy of my feeling is easily wasted in the loud fury. Oh, scotch the repugnant for the rills of the moon are upon us. But I am nothing more than a freak of nature. Come to me, I call out! I must write to beat the devil. Here I stand alone meddling with the dominion of good and evil. Oh, the untold hours of misery, study, and mental exhaustion. It is plain to see that I suffer from such vehemence.

With my astonishment there was

something in the distance that snapped like a fresh carrot. Things were beginning to happen! I walked mechanically down the thoroughfare in a daze so unlike my happiness at dinner earlier. Everything changed from being such a delight to a rending despair in a matter of moments. I needed a drink, something quite toxic, and I ducked into a sleepy-looking bar. It was impossible to arouse any of the patrons so deeply self-indulgent were they? Nonetheless, the liquor seemed to pick up my spirits and I departed longing for light and the fresh air. I mused about my self portraiture and a poem which were coming along quite well. In fact, they were growing like an adventitious vine with the netherworld at my heels. But to be truthful they are merely portraits of suffering and of a secrecy that would not be nudged into the light. If my story was only exquisitely told!

Nonetheless the damned 'unnamable' of these warring parties is elusive and leaves me brooding on these holidays.

In the distance my poor neighbor lady was weeping to break my heart and thus I entered into the triumvirate: the ringing of my ears, a noise like a swarm of bees, and beneath it all the patter of words and mischief. It would seem that anything is enough to set this cascade off. That is, my thoughts sounding off like a busy kitchen. Not far off the sea naturally wallows beneath the clouds and she sidles by me until there arrives the fugitive ghosts of the sea. The resounding clap of the waters, the hiss of the sea rolls in like serpents.

Yes, one must wait for true companions among this enormous entourage. Sooner or later I shall hum the dove's song like a sad but pretty anthem. Each night, tired and nearly penniless, I fall to sleep. Still, I was obliged to see myself through it all and, in fact, in hindsight I was invincible. In these more recent days I am in fair humor. One might say that I am even cheerful no matter what the curious circumstances. With a hammer I shall strike the bell and come out fighting while the fires roar! To stay the game was my honor and my highest achievement.

The limits of my nature were indeterminate. The written word was not worth an ounce of my trials. At home I light the candles ensconced above the Buddha's head. In the damp gardens little lamps scout the way. They shone and rattle inside me as if they were the wind in the rafters of my small home. Add to this that the chimes are ringing in the fateful breeze. Tonight I shall tramp until I am exhausted. Inwardly, I grope for my strength. This entire affair, this way of life has the gorse of my hair standing on end. Soon I must attain some form of tranquility or perish. With style and discretion to these scalloped ramparts I find my tongue.

I must practice methodical doubt. Upon the table veined with marble I must remark about the blank pages of this diary. And with these troubles I must collaborate no matter how wretched be my fate. My lazy habitus is radiant with ambiguous feelings and caprice. Today, at the repertory of voices, I feel an inertia that is not so very disagreeable. How may I assist this dragging of my feet? What vulgar stimulus goads them? Why despair over these agonies?

Sometimes the sirens beneath the waters summon my attention. In this connection nothing could blight the breadth of my understanding. Above me there lies a cluster of stars. Beside me are the rustling of leaves. Below me I shudder with the cold and damp. Where in this kingdom do I belong? What course should I sow? What relations should I sunder?

How could an agency, any agency, usurp the judicial rights of an individual? In my bewilderment, let it be known, I sought for serenity and acquittal. My coteries of 'good' and 'evil' are fanning out, my mouth is agape, the manacles are tightly turded. My youth has quietly disappeared as well as most of middle age. I must continue to write, to hammer in exhaustion. For goodness sakes these underlings are ransacking my soul with their jagged and chthonian world. It must be remembered that long ago I had given up reading books, and hence the boredom I sustained, to write for my pleasure.

Today is littered with voices and the fermentation of the crowd surrounds me.

However, chivalrous is my manner as the birds are in flight. The sky has been breached as it sits in wonderment. And I, I am merely in search of safer climes. It is the magnitude of my dilemma that exacerbates my patience. Are my efforts too truculent for understanding? Who, after all, was I going to swindle with the alphabet? To bustle and scurry twelve years of my life - alas! And tonight, once again, I will run tired and panting all the way home.

Please permit me to hang upon Pindar's words: "Oh, my soul, do not aspire to immortality but exhaust the limits of the possible." Still it is not without the sweat of my brow that I tramp the streets. In what sounds like a vast hallway I exude my feelings, my gallery proofs, my gut. It is no secret that madmen finish last, they don't finish at all! Left to its own device this mad, psychotic devil, this foreign principle will seize me by the throat and cast me from the heights to the sea. But in this connection I must go happily reconciled like Sisyphus. As it is said, "one must imagine Sisyphus happy." Add to this that "in life we are all beginners" and you have the essence of the equation. Looking into the universal waters of the sea I now address the upward moon slipping into the quay as quiet as an hourglass. Perhaps soon I will grow to understand this flying chase. For conspiring against me my mind is racked to perpetuity.

Returning home I sit quietly upon the landing smoking and deliberating. Am I a soldier? Have I thus taken leave of my senses? I try to hold them at bay as I register the pulse of my allies, my wayside optimism. Keen sighted and free they led the way, as a pilgrimage into the distance and futurity. What aesthete considerations yield to me with honor and respect? Carrying on as I do you would think that I write indelible scriptures in the sky. But behold! I long to cry out from deep in my heart. However, this cris d'coeur fails to summon any ol' pals, acquaintances, any type of worthy company. Still if you would prick up your ears you, too, could hear the voices and ejaculations coming from afar to settle in the conch of your ears. Are they direct threats or companioned figures of my soul? It is quite clear that usually they emanate from the veils of the sea. This much was sure and certain! Equally so, I must make good my plans and calculations, snubbing the intrusions about me.

Nibbling at the cuffs of my jacket I turn to a blank wall. Gladly I would trade places with any old fool. When, I wondered, was the government going to show itself and make a statement to myself and the court. Did the government perhaps think of me as guilty of some heinous form of sedition? Maybe with time we could merely laugh it off as some great and grand artifice, a case of legerdemain, so to speak. If this was my situation I would do well to offer them nosegay and a pinch of chewing tobacco and send them on their merry way.

Obviously I have need of my day in court. One tires of comminatory words and the formidable hunt. Would anything change? After all, I could very well be injured or dead and nobody would raise a hand, or so it would seem.

At the bay this morning the wharves were empty but for the bright bunting, a few riggings, beach towels, and swimming gear. Everyone was set out to sea under the deepening blue skies while the meniscus of the moon faded to nothing. The breathtaking waters sat motionless except for the ruffles bobbing this grand still life. Then it came time to doze and I beat it back home to my solitary room. Outside the windows the arbors waved their branches in the breeze while I closed my eyes resigning myself to sleep.

In the midst of a nightmare I awoke and lumbering to my feet I clenched my fists and shook my arms at the ochre colored sky, mounting an assault of my own. Then grumbling and cursing I threw myself back into bed awaiting a more gentle sleep.

Later, unable to sleep, I ambled in the cool morning to the park alone and wept openly well deserved tears. Flinching with every breath I muzzled my hurt, my discomfort, and my pain. To town I crept becoming a part of the great throng of people. Yes, the light brush of people made sweethearts of my soul. Even a hermit deserves some touch and affection. After all, he has his code of honor.

I must rise from this River Styx without anymore pretty speeches. In efforts of great candor I talk to myself from beneath the scurrying clouds and I dawdle away the hours. Always forced to attend to the veils of whispers in the distance I accordingly advance or retreat. However, possessed or not I must insist upon being absolved of culpability in all crimes. Of labyrinthine difficulty its course mirrors my own peril upon these lawless roads.

Soon conditions will prevail that will filch the last of my possessions. I can well digest the fact, it being of no consequence. But will I be pardoned, pardoned from the curse of these animosities? Flooded by unseen casualties any benign party might wring their hands of me, banish me for once and for all. Or might they be stiffened by an oblique and trouncing insult. One, let us say, invented to exhaust their patience of me. But usually equivocal and uncertain these terms good and evil issue from one common and universal source.

At the gleaming of the sea today I took an astounded vigil at the promontory. I could almost envision the sailors and the sirens all raising hell. Would they soon be coming for me? The few lights upon the bay are illustrious and I feel esteemed by the atmosphere in general. But was I duped by an irony that I failed to see? For at the same time I felt dreadfully tired to my very roots. Stung by this solitude and fatigue I ambled home to pour myself a good, long drink. On the way, led by the flickering lights, I took notice once again of the crowds and their communications. Cell phones in the hands of every civilian, cars turning in all directions fanned the streets and the hillsides making way for myself wherever I traversed. Nobody was either friendly or not friendly. Nobody was available for counsel or for disputation. The virulence of their bitter indifference cast me into a mold to which I objected, but one that I would have to endure. Nothing is enlightening in either the rustling of the trees or the glimmering sea. It is neither the sea nor the trees that bear responsibility and believe me nobody gains from the pith of our clandestine arguments. However sometimes either of these miscreants or the benevolent party would present themselves as delightful rogues. It would appear that perhaps keeping me down or lifting me up was their hobby and their vocation. Nonetheless I clearly enough

wasn't going to give up and I wasn't going to give in. I was adamant. My fists were made of iron. I would never abdicate nor in my skull would I lose my aspiring will. Alas, my despair will be all that I possess. Surrender, it wasn't in my blood!

VII

My entire life pales to this condition of survival. My entire life! As usual I look for charges from which I am to be exonerated. Of course without avail. Like cattle I am branded and made ready for the slaughterhouse. I only have to gently walk through 'the valley of death' to at last be exculpated from accusations that flood my way. What judge could mediate this disaster, this disorder, this plague? Blushing from the chilly air I scuttle through a town whose streets will perhaps

110

be my new home.

Among the trees silhouettes rise and fall like my breathing and I reply to the voices with austerity - I shall make my life work! I feel that whatever the opposition I will be at the summit of my powers. Though I loathe the inconvenience of certain chores when homeless there is candor and simplicity and immediacy with which to approach a problem if one exists. 'Keep it clear and simple' I reply with gratitude. 'Clear and simple!'

As a tramp I become acquainted, once again, with the cool disposition of these occult societies that both, good and evil, pullulate in great throngs. The pungent language of my antagonists has me reeling with confusion. The irrepressible nature of this discourse has me delivering soliloquies of my own. Frequently the party befriending me would rejoice at the substance of my chit-chat. Though enormous drifts of denunciatory words showered about me the good and natural impetus of my allies (whoever they are) infected me with laughter and a superabundance of comedic material.

From the peninsula I can see the vitreous body of the ocean standing quite still and then wallowing expansively. Soon the quarrelsome prattle of my enemies will surge into a death blow. Still I must be grateful for the times that I was in fine feather. Yes, milling about the herd I can feel the forces of being doggedly pursued. Awkward, but not altogether tactless, appear the ejaculations of this nemesis. Resounding with a horrible boom they insist upon capturing me and my full attention. An unwitting patron of both camps I have only to bide my time. I am feeling festive in the glistening rain. A sweetish fragrance appears, imaginatively, as tea in a gold-inlaid cup. Amused and curious I leap over the little puddles of a side street. There is no need to retort to my nemesis who have, incidentally, vanished for what reason only the powers that be know. I am thirsty and I open my mouth to capture the falling rain then I stop at the water fountain to fill my bottle. The horizon is dusky. Soon the light will fail and everything will be lost to sight. At bedtime I begin to wonder if I will be visited by complex dreams as the other night.

Chattering in the twilight I dare these other forces to challenge me. At the same time I shrink from such duty and I count my blessings. For I know that these voices from another world will not pale altogether. In fact it is a secret covenant that they shall stay, almost without interruption, by my side as long as my heart beats. I am certain that they were secretly administering dope, as I have mentioned, but I do not know by what methods this was attained. No matter how long I beat my head no information was forthcoming. Tonight one crushing blow after another issued forth as if from some great monolith. Even the meniscus of the moon was ever so haunting. Haunting enough to make me wail in tears by the evening black cypresses absent of all people but for a lone sheriff.

Chanting mysterious and unrecognizable verse I hastened to home. Choking on tears I pressed my head to the pillow swearing off all humanity. I climbed out of bed to close the shutters upon the world. Then I dove back upon my sleeping bag for warmth. Suddenly I felt the need to peer into a mirror. There I discovered the crises in my reflection. Yes, facing me I could register their tireless rant knowing no bounds. Hence, I feel doomed in a way that I have never before known. Think! I cry out. But should I call my plan, a stupid plan, clever? That is, if I had one.

It is clearly upon me to shake the tree for its fruit. I must not abdicate entirely. I must give my undivided vigil and study the complete absorption of my mind. Nothing else will suffice. Whether or not the law comes calling for me, whether or not I have my day in court is of less consequence than originally conceived. For the workings of my mind have been thoroughly challenged, and with the defiance put to me, I will no longer march in single file. The value of their hideous banter breeds only more patience within myself and I shall remain in good form to the last ounce of my strength.

It is no use raving over minor plans, propositions, or antiquated theorems. The deeper truth be known, it will be of no consequence how our obituaries read. The point is to live and be happy. As if there was no other life, past or future.

Last night I was spellbound and while the stars flickered in their glass casements the river plunged down into the sea. This morning the wind is up and the sea is furious, whipping as of leather. I arrive here after vacating my last hovel.

The shrubbery at the far side of the office buildings makes a perfect haunt for myself and my few belongings. For the drizzle I don a big, blue tarp which seems to hold the water at bay as does the little thatched roof of the anteroom to one of the shops.

I rub my hands together as if I was by a fire and commence to write a poem. It must be something horrible, shocking, and barbaric as has been their dealings with me.

It is, of course, with this truculence that I must intend to reproduce the natural and unnatural settings and characters with whom I have met. It is no small objective, nonetheless, if I could only practice patience I might very well be onto something worthwhile. But I am dealing with a pendulum now that I purposely wished to lose. I am frightened that this project will never rise to any height nor will it plunge into the depths of my soul and its wanderings.

Today was a surprisingly good day. I swear to you, the silence, the blessed silence was nearly absolute! What more or less could sweeten the kitty so? I have before coiled and recoiled, advanced and receded. But today was something else, unctuous as soil, and spirited with great ardor. The quintessence of silence seemed to sit inside of me, unabashed by the greatest of noises.

The gray and miserly rain hasn't taken hold and I beg to swoon to all of creation. This thin rain is beginning to boil my blood. I suppose I will soon fade into the backdrop and I will become a ragman or a hobo. However, I will continue to grow even in this inauspicious setting. It is no longer up to me to puzzle over conundrums of those about me. We are make believe. We are living things. We are dreaming things coming of age at different times. If I have to creep I will. If I have to wax with the fantastic I will. If I have to drive, forcing the nail, I will.

It would appear that I am somehow repugnant to all others. As I have said, not so much as a glance has grazed me in some years. And so I am this hermit sauntering down the cool esplanade to the foot of the cliff where I will pitch camp only to eat a meager meal of nuts and bread and wine.

Yes, my crowned kingdom has been razed by half-wit speculations and considerable impatience. Still, one must keep looking for clues to my pursuit. Perhaps, though I am no thief, it to me to force a lock or two. Either for the staff of life or a dwelling where I might find peace. As for these two rivaling factions I must continue to ask; by what methods do they track and trail me? How do they siphon these drugs into my frail system? Nonetheless it is an absurd conclusion that I might derive some clear and sustaining home truth where there is none. One can see that I never tire of putting a picture in a frame no matter how askew.

Occasionally, I will nod to a citizen to summon their attention. In spite of my efforts seldom are matters reciprocated. A simple gesture would suffice. But no! Instead everyday is a solemn occasion, nothing dear implied, nothing soluble in the works.

In this secret and grandiose litigation overwhelming me now the vast legal officialdom has been set loose. Preying upon me I am entirely without counsel. Imagine that! With great solitude I am aware that if I properly asserted myself and I was triumphant above and beyond my bashfulness that my deliverance would be swift and final. Nevertheless, falling out of favor from the human race was more than a small hurdle to leap. I leave it only to imagination to consummate this redeeming act not knowing any longer how to orchestrate desire and tenderness. Oh, but with this frame corrected I should be uxorious to a fault with the midwifery of my prose leading the way.

I must finally bow out retiring from any purpose of blame or censure. It is simple to make accusations when your world is no more than a pitching sea in which to expire. With good fortune I will not again be dragged to rave before the stars and by the sea. There are plentiful tears and maledictions for those that sew the great commissure between myself and others. It is a border, perhaps, that should never be crossed. I notice that these grave questions no longer exert their influence or power when you are among friends. In fact, they are laughable and conform merely to tolerance. To be sure, I no longer need anymore quarrelsome company until my last gasp of air. I need to make of the sea a shrine as agile as its parting hands.

Somewhere the tasteless gossip has been wrested and the marmoreal seagulls stand like sentries. Among this little heap of consecration I deliberate, turn mute, and sigh. The dazzling light implores me so.

Soon commend me and we will indulge in a canter or two. No need for melancholy, the insufferable, or formality as stiff as buckram. But I am getting drowsy by the lithesome waters that lay so voluptuously. Such luxuries are free. Such gifts accompanied me in youth and are promising to entertain me and reinvent me into my future and my feebleness. Stand tall, so be it! What shall I do for an encore? Very wisely I shall do nothing. My arrest and judicial proceedings, I suppose, will come soon or not at all. And I have no doubt that, if proceedings take place, I will be vindicated.

But the sea, she is lovely this morning, shuttling in from the four corners of the world! However, all too soon, seething madness would ring out under a myriad of stars. This clay, this year, is no wiser than what went before. The torrents still rundle from the heavens, the leaves flash in the breeze, and consequently I cozy in. Meanwhile I take to pounding out and hammering a story worth the telling. Oh, how it remains to be seen, this tale of a runabout.

For it was this tale that would lead me to new heights and grant to me citizenship in the world.

VIII

Tonight the streets are silent and empty. I sit by my little room on the stoop. I am dreaming up inquiries to resurrect myself and my hopes of more authorship. I have stumbled upon a book of publishing houses and literary agents at the library to appease such hopes and I choose those that appear to be best suited for my proposals and query letters thus far. It is necessary that to become successful I will have to collect myself and banish these curses striking me from my blind side. I will have to burn my candle at both ends, as they say, and I shall have to give up the ghost for conduct that arises now from force of habit as much as any creative well that I might harbor. However, in this connection my understanding is sometimes opaque. It is becoming a challenge to insinuate my innocence at the risk of losing my audience and my heart, likewise, is heavy with sorrow. In the expanse that lays before me I will go quietly, softly without ceremony. Still, I feared that this heart, cumbrous with misfortune, would be the end of me. With what afflictions upon my shoulders do I make these travels? With what shall I despise them and corner them for my bidding? I must go like the wind and flatter myself along the way. At times, it would seem, that my gaiety was running riot while

I coddled these words. But mind you there was something insufferable in this board game. In this regard I must embrace the demure that stands contrary to these insults and buoy myself with a sunny disposition. I wouldn't allow my manners to become coarse and vulgar. I would become more discreet with my behavior and drive contempt, not humility, from the fields of my inquiry.

A woman passes by me to enter her abode and I couldn't help noticing that her eyes were quite livid. What I have done to deserve this wrath is uncertain. Perhaps it was time to strike a bargain but my greeting was met with derision and she seemed almost joyous in making a mockery of my efforts. Still there was no need to fret. I would attempt to summon a compromise with the proper adjustments.

Why was it that I always wore my

125

heart on my sleeve? To stifle my conscience and my ethical sense I merely shrug my shoulders and conjure a laugh. It was clear that she was capable of a brutality that was foreign to most of her young age. With what do I entreat her on bended knees? I begged her as I begged mankind and she showed me no mercy. Why shouldn't she with good will come forth on my behalf? Toward her my back was against the wall and I was, I could see, in a world of trouble. It was heartrending, to be sure, but there was no need to be cross, I counseled myself. It was second nature to fall back on my strengths, though with age, they seemed to be fading.

She departed without saying as much as a word and passed out of sight down the darkened hallway. In the sky sparrows darted through space. Coerced by her rudeness I discovered myself rising to go upstairs to my room. I poured myself a glass of tea and began to write odes about the friendly soul that I was without. Beyond fabrication I would yield to my imagination distant yet discrete. And there I would tempt providence with a fling of my own, crisp and fresh. Was it by chance that my inventions came so easily? Out of necessity and longing as the case may be. Sometimes these spoiled words were merely the product of trying one's luck whether or not my story was credible or not. At least it was a worthwhile escape from suffering those about me, the deceivers and cheats alike. Soon the darkness fell and I climbed into bed. Before sleep took me I asked myself 'would I spend the entirety of my days, this impermanence amidst only troublesome times?' Or would I successfully strive to remedy my cause and come about brimming with joy? Thus far I have wasted myself; it must be said, with the bosh of a simpleton. But should I submit to this guileless and good faith counting on a reprieve for my efforts. I would stop at nothing to land a clearing with which I might growl at these devils and succor my pleasures to come. Oh, but sometimes the middle road that I ventured was aggravating and made me quite irritable. Here I longed for thunder in my words and the hunger of great promise. It was time to dramatize my surroundings with an exuberant reply. Perhaps, I thought, I might scurry off to a theater where I would disgust the audience with my antics and verify with memory my sordid past. Better yet I could very well imagine management throwing me out to the opposition of grateful spectators who would be shouting with appreciation for my lurid interruptions and my striking interpretations. That's it! I would take them all by surprise. Moreover I would impart that which I cherished in these otherwise stagnant waters. I would revere the good traits of my brothers and sisters that, even though they were not patent in stature, had seen me through some of my more difficult days. They were, no doubt, extraordinary in number and even more remarkable in their skills. However, my inveterate shyness prevented me from any such exploits and as I raced through the park in this declining and miserable state I rifled through my pockets for any forgotten change. My stomach was distended, empty with nothing but water and my hunger had me on the brink of vomiting. I was no longer magnanimous but selfish instead. Nonetheless, despite my many flaws, I remained, under the circumstances, somewhat amicable.

I sat on a bench at the far end of the park, rubbing my stomach, trying to calm down from this distressed condition. Close by a vagrant, not unlike myself, played an old and beaten guitar. He had his case opened next to him, presumably for gratuities. But as I approached him I could see that it was empty. I nodded my head and forced a smile. He reciprocated and I felt a strange kinship of poverty and loss. As I had no money I couldn't very well tip him and I was sure that this he understood. As a consequence I turned suddenly and I sauntered toward home. I was fairly certain that I might still have a crust of bread. Something I had forgotten in my knapsack when I had recycled a few cans and bottles the day before. Such was the luck of my recollection. It was like a gift, one that had been forgotten, and I devoured it as best I could though my digestion left something to be desired. I managed to coat my stomach from the acids gnawing at me the entire day and lay down to rest. From my hunger I was becoming more and more fatigued. Among other things I realized that, my greeting the man in the park was the only time I had spoken to another in days. Hence my writing began to summon me in more imperious ways. There was an element of truth that this self-restrained solitude contributed to my efforts of authorship and it appeared that the only form of justice that I could pursue was to write without pause. Toward this end I stormed out of my room bent on cashing in on more bottles and cans. My reasoning was thus, to buy a few groceries so that I might stay in my wretched dwelling and write to my heart's content without any interruptions whatsoever. I positively beamed at this proposition dreaming up new material and axioms to abide by in this insidious row that lay at my doorstep.

I lit one of many cigarette ends that I had found on the trail to the ash cans, refuse containers and the grocery store and entered my lodging to encamp with my labor of love. I was obliged by these gestures that netted me a good find of recyclable cans and I was struck by the clarity of my thoughts to write no matter what the sacrifice or penalty or path to my spirits may be. I was pressing on good strides to avoid a stale and lifeless outcome and to spare my wits of an austere conclusion. Diversions and amusements would spin me like a top though I retreated with good form to coerce what seemed to be the inevitable. Sweet memories of my trysts and conquests were beginning to get the upper hand and I sported this fund of knowledge for all to see. I was clearly avoiding the society of others now and with this gesture striking a pose from the wastelands of my solitude. I found no resentment nor bitterness in my inventions, only simplicity and a certain fondness for my affairs and characters alike. Presumably this could not last. But for the present enthusiasm and passion were turning me inside out. Though there would soon be obstructions to deceive me. I was presently having great exultation in my struggles.

From my window I watched the horizon looming with clouds in the distance and I could espy the woman from yesterday. I could see that she was up to no good, spreading displeasure and being always somewhere else in her mind. At least she wasn't meddling in my private matters. Of course I was repulsed by her conduct but I would make a conscious effort to avoid her no matter what lengths I had to traverse. Unlike her, despite my many flaws, I remained genial and good natured. I discovered that whatever remembrances stood before me my spirits were lifted. Nevertheless, was I sound of mind and clever or foolish and absurd? What substance, devoid of mirth, would impart pleasure? None! Or was there something of happiness to be had anyway?

Next to my little room was another woman. However, contrary to the woman whom I met with some objection, she was modest and presented herself with a meekness that didn't do justice to her intelligence nor her apparent sensibilities. As much as I wanted to wash my hands of the former I wished to accept the latter without protest or criticism. Perhaps some day soon we would meet and carry on with a lively discussion. After all, one should be animated from time to time. In other words writing would have to cease now and then for the gift of gab and warmth of rubbing shoulders. But for now life was nothing more than a holiday, writing sometimes at breakneck speed. Imprisoning myself in my room was the fitting and scrupulous thing to do. Nonetheless, I must ask, what was behind this mask of some subterfuge in which I had thrown myself? For at times, ennui and weariness would envelop me without warning. For a moment I would fall silent then, before I knew it, I would turn abruptly with a vengeance, scribbling almost like a madman, but one still possessed with some of his faculties. Yes, exquisite were my terms as I snatched at the dialogue concussing at my door. At such times I felt that my muse would never desert me. Oh, heavens this world beyond did reign about me. But rather than noble and selfless I was often selfish and insignificant, as when I was young. To be sure, once I was a young man, stylish and lean. Everyday and all day long was a Saturday and a lazy afternoon by the sea. Then I would have my share of romance sleeping with one woman after the other without discrepancy. I would invoke poetry and invent words that were not without magnetism and constraint and the bedroom was never too far off. I was an avid suitor that was without equal. Meanwhile women flaunted themselves without hesitation.

The next morning I was strutting, making progress with the itinerary that I had laid out the night before. These would prove to be the toys and trifles I would have at my disposal to pass the time of day. I dealt conceit with every budding syllable and crowed with a callous behavior unbecoming to me. But I began to grow wary of the brotherhood that would see me through this solitude.

It was the third day of my self imposed imprisonment and, with the rising temperature; eternal fire seemed to hang from my window. I drank greedily one iced tea after another. I saw to it that my fictions would stir the innocence or guilt of these matters at hand. With the proper touch of humor and amusement I would handle, as in youth, the task of celebrating guilt and innocence alike. I would boast of the solace and comfort of my fellow subordinates that I would crush or put down with the right words. With scorn I would curl my lips at the just opprobrium to this end. I would knock about my room sparing no insults and I would, with inwardness, bless or curse my opponents robbed of their efficacy by my economy with words. At times I felt as though I was close to putting down my last words and then, without warning, there arose an excess of ideas that would make many green with envy and spiteful as well.

However, as I looked into the mirror I could see that I was growing corpulent from lethargy. Hence I decided against former convictions to stay put and to take a long walk downtown. With the heat I was stewing now more conscious of the enigma that followed me to and fro. I could see this smokescreen and through it the sophistry of the public that crowded the streets.

What the hell, I said to myself; I shall grin and bear it. I will endure this ruse into the future. Whether or not the many uncertainties are explicable or not means nothing. What judgment and ruling, what acumen and shrewdness would press me to the wall finding in me a worthy opponent of their diatribes. As I have said many times over my character and pose was, perhaps curious, but nevertheless, without question. Unassailable I would persevere with great virtue. No accusations ventured nor verdict made I was shut up in my little world free to come and go as I saw fit. And yet the liberties of this chase were made under duress without precedence as well as without surcease. The omnipresence of these devils was clear regardless of their obscurity in form, pattern, and design. But moreover I have vowed not to trespass their perimeters no matter how nameless or unsung. I would conduct myself with a seeming conviction and ardor that few possessed. I must write to justify my life, a life tampered with by nearly every passer-by. I would stroll with these 'good' people down memory lane. I would go down the long boulevard filled with former assignations and performances unrivaled. I would storm this town that lay like the river

Styx. Once this seemed to be the harbinger of a bright future but it proved to be one that was never to be born. It is true that my post in life left something to be desired, nonetheless, I was adamant about a deserving conclusion.

Before my subjects knew it they would be smarting from a thwack in the head. For my words were sometimes quite brutal no matter how superficial they may have sounded to be from the outset. However, my melancholy that often interfered seemed perpetual in scope and alas got the best of me on many occasions. In this regard I would hobble and flounder for a quick reprieve from these demons and dolorous moods. But as time goes on the gloom and despair of a heavy heart, sullen in its cage, debilitates me more and more and soon, I fear, I will be lost altogether. Though my belongings and valuables are few my tastes are nevertheless extravagant. Once I had lived a fairly prosperous life with as many riches as any fellow could desire. But now those days are over and the truth be known I don't miss them one iota. More importantly how would I cope with this wilderness of sorts? I find the present to be a mystery, unsolved and grueling at times. I am struggling for food and shelter and trying to land the product of my 'big book.' I was abundantly preoccupied but equally terrified that I wouldn't be able to pull it off in the end.

I hastened to make short work of my project and to incite providence and forethought prudently. To lose oneself in the creation of this book, to siphon fate, and to gamble with chance for my prize was my philosophy. To this end my gratitude would soar. If I failed my future, I feel, will be oblivion and the void that crushes its victim without pause. At this bidding I would have to summon, I see, all my strength. But rather than becoming guilty of dissecting my abominable adversaries I would do best to lead them by the scruff of the neck. Moreover, if I was to flourish I would have to first make a judicious effort of my cunning against, and effacement of, this netherworld.

I see this clearly, in the palm of my hands, what frustrates and inhibits my efforts to conquer this underworld. What issues forth is a bogus and impenetrable cry of my own, one that fails to pierce one's ears. Rather than rapping their skulls with my knuckles I would do well to beckon from the depths of myself the fondness I feel for conjuring up a line of defense toward these villains. If I was to persist I must stop at nothing to achieve a coherent whole and to throw off the scent of these devilish others.

Perhaps some day soon, before they knew it, they would be left with nothing to preside over. As pleasing as this may sound I was still somewhat blinded and unconscious of their hold upon me. When it came to penetrating me with their sonar I was divided in my temperament. With what other devises were they prepared to strike? Were they prepared to permit something attractive and flattering to nudge me out of their corner they might have discovered a more pleasing side of me. But no, I wheeze at their suggestions that are never too unclouded.

As if that isn't confounding enough what about their skill in addressing my so-called infirmity. It is an infirmity, an illness, I would never have guessed. My brain was no more than a map of their excursions oftentimes and oftentimes it was difficult to invoke a rite of passage from their stranglehold. Something noble, something where I can come into my own was too far away today and my only recourse was to inveigh these devils surrounding me. At this juncture I compare their contempt with my own. The tumult that dispossesses me of sanity is muddled and nonplussed. Thus I must blot out and suppress every one of their intentions without exception.

After all they were the aggressors in these trials. They would never say die, they would never take 'no' for an answer. Still I remained the exemplar, the ideal, immune from prosecution. In the meanwhile the figures and silhouettes came dancing before me with an impudence unequivocal thus far.

Part Two

I

The genie of my computer reveals
nothing but a blank stare. It is up to me to
extirpate the distant silhouettes. The
spillways, the cisterns, the gutters and the
sluice gates gurgle beneath me, above me
the blond azure. Entrenched by the
battlements of my castle walls, what of my
spiritual situs, what of memory has been
sustained? To wish for the flaming and
bronze statuary of autumn's fire and not the
flamboyancy of my wanton prose. Fall, the
mistress of melancholy! One must hope for
the best and open your eyes to the throng of
stars and commiserate. Oh! To pass
through the little embers, I may not be
anybody! Will I turn to stone beneath

thunderous cries and excitability or will I be resurrected, fusing my skull and spine, disabusing me of these images? Must I clamber up the cathedral walls to become the bell ringer? All of these thoughts passed by me in an instant. Again, to stifle my tongue, to shut forever my eyes, I sometimes longed for my departure.

However, in the autumn the gold, enameled leaves scurry along the walks, merely a dimple of fall. But the traditions of this season are boisterous, beige and burgundy and the flakes of yellow leaves sweeping the pavement. And what of the colossal shadows, the lull before the storm! Yes, at the crown of the mountain the skies were breached. In the meantime, the brush of autumn's leaves against the paving held me grieving in precipitous silence.

With the massive shoulders of the sea, I bare my chest. Oh, madness, oh despair, oh shepherds bringing in the shadows, cleaving the hillocks of green pastures to a death knoll! I wandered upon the edge of the world, upon the horizon, blushed by the heavens and anointed with tears. And there I staved off the madness encircling me. And there I watched the glittering waters, sorrow hanging in the balance. Nonetheless, what has happened to the portal of my being and the portentous shadows of my soul? What was this ominous clatter-trap upon my shoulders? Why, I could barely speak! Lost are the days of innocence, rational and clear reasoning untouchable. You stir your impatience among the gardens scribbling in your dog-eared text. There you wept not for yourself, but for the sake of humanity! It was a condition that would haunt me for years! One that would sweeten the kitty of rude confessions. A necessary passage, a rite to succeed, would I tread thus on thee? Character, dialogue, and scenic purple passages, I am none of these. Then who am I? Am I merely a recluse begging for time?

And so I creep, thinning out the text as time unfolds. Meanwhile, the leaves are skating on the cold ground while I lay pale and exhausted. The banalities of the cities languish among the stars. The metronome was clocking out my time. I could feel it in my bones as an arthritic can feel the rain in his joints.

Forgive me for now but the spell of the moon has me quite tethered. Oh, he, my fool, imaginary or not bounded forth in colorful ribbons, spouting truce. Stop! To pillage through this lame composition has me miserable. But beneath a blue sky the sun shivered in the great hall of the soul that addressed, presented itself patent and radiant. The fall was so brief, so final, and the advent of winter would soon appear.

I arose this morning naked and vulnerable to the sea, to the staggered and reeling rhythms of the sea. It wasn't too long before my heart grew lighter as, from a waggish exclamation, and the first such circumstances in several months was born. Even though the tides beat at my torso with solicitations, I swam into a quiet cove to discover a solitary eel. There, it seemed, I was the spokesman for my own fate while the blessed sea rocked me in its cradle, rocked me like a child in its arms. Further off the waves were landing with a thunderous clap. But what of this loneliness that has visited me and why is there this raw infatuation with autumn? What of this infrared cell of fall? Moreover why not strike with noble wit instead of letting a vein.

Myself, the reluctant hero, the essence

of the fantastic, divested of the fringes, of the fanciful, of the picturesque. Of these we have jubilated! At the dear interim I hobbled back and forth. The instincts were deeply embedded and my anguish and apprehension did not persist. It must be remembered that I did not falter when I was humored. And so I winced inwardly at the endless sea. I made silent preparations for my return from the quay. When I regarded the text, my text, I cried from my breast the vagaries of destiny. My shabby self to wither on the stalk. The fall leaves were shaking like pages ripped from a fat book. Once again I was a runabout. As I walked I could feel this book writing itself! These ragged but living memoirs were coming together very handsomely. Accordingly, I addressed the horizon thankfully and moved on. At home, even though it was a sunny morning I, for some unknown reason, kept the doors and windows closed and locked. I was thus imprisoned, but without rage or rant or monstrous dimension. It was a shade different from returning with the public that seemed to crowd around me like a twin fetus in the womb. But mine was to thrust myself between waking reality and the dream and to cipher the results! The world must be more pleasant, I thought. Nonetheless, there is little timid about her.

Night has fallen and the constellations hang like vineyards in the sky. But I am weary and I must stop this fatuous and wretched mind. For some reason I began to recall summer roses. Probably it was memory of love and its endearments but I couldn't really say. However, it is true that I carried my years well even though there were many sunless horizons. In other words, nights without love. Perhaps I owed my youth to expunging my body and soul of its dross with words. Oh, but I remember I could smell the locks of her hair. Her neck was redolent with perfume. Behind her arms and knees lay the utmost sweetness. It was the must of her limbs that captured me. But for now my true love must now become my pen, however poor, however great.

I am here to bear the elation of invention and the ideal! Henceforth, I blunder listless into the irony of stares and premonitions. Angels in the twilight, I peer with sheer and youthful exuberance, angling toward the proud night. My eyes, to this day, rest upon an undying love. Nevertheless, in love, as in authorship, I am improvident lacking both foresight and substance. Oh! What agony and pain we suffer. I wish, above all, to settle down and to break these chains. For, as I have said, I am young at heart and my heart lies with autumn and is an heir of its lovely sadness. All of this is engineered by the fleece of the breakers at shore. Ah! To savor one's dreams, of simplicity and of beauty. Shrouded not by the clouds is the night's wind and the autonomy of the sky. Perhaps we will one day meet with a measure of good fortune and unrequited love!

In the meadows, in a dark and abandoned garage, I let my thoughts incubate. Slowly my eyes began to adjust themselves to a passage of thin light that came through the door that was ajar landing upon a shovel, a wheelbarrow, and a crude pitchfork. The quiet lent itself to a certain calm and peace with which to judge the present circumstances. But while the lighting was serving itself up as a deliberate and simple beauty I began to fall into irreparable melancholy. Would this trouble brewing sustain me even if I was only able to paint thumbnail sketches? Despite objections this miserable volume was raising its head as it should be. That is, even though it suffered and sobbed as it did so. Perhaps I find the need to encompass the rhythms of yesterday. It is an aesthetic means of pursuit but I don't want to argue the point. My intentions are worthy of themselves. But it leads me to the conclusion that all is not well. Meanwhile, illusory promises befriend me. The sympathetic eyes, the sweeping hand gestures, lo and behold should there be anymore of this scaffolding laid. I must still carry the skill to adapt to the aesthetic rules no matter how unruly! At this crossing it is silly, isn't it, to wave humor as a bastion for the soul? And yet humor comes to my mind.

Why, the other day, walking past a

154

beach party, I remembered something that made me grow curious and upset. There was a conversation that I overheard presumably about my precarious condition. I believe the word, paranoid, was used to describe me. Nevertheless I could not make out many more morsels than this and I soon relinquished my post at the seamark hustling away from their chat. But the light that befriended me here in the garage was, like my thoughts, all but snuffed out. My predisposition was to vanish before the mantle of darkness like a resplendent bird, mystified by disbelief of my compatriot's words at the party. It made no sense to rob me of my peace of mind. Yet, rob me, they did! "Spare me this curse" I offered up to the sky, "spare me," I rallied toward my cause. But no reply was forthcoming.

I must have nodded off for I emerged from a deep sleep with a start. So fresh was my dream that I could recall its content to the centimeter. It was about a French woman who roamed the coastal streets. Her pale legs and face, her bright lips and jewelry, her constant, dissociated chatter reigned over this twilight. I was quick to discover that she was a Parisian uprooted from her home. However, this dream was actually a distant memory of a reality that I once knew and shone as bright as a colored sail in the sun. Why it had visited me, of a sudden, was an enigma. But to tell the truth I felt blessed, such an aegis shining in my corner amidst this awful solitude. In the distance was the clamorous ringing, the peal of giant bells, and to this music I walked swiftly back to home.

No amount of worry would distress me. I was tired and growing incurious to everything about me. And with the certitude that is confidence I soon dozed off once again.

I awoke from this resignation and slackened my thirst with the bathroom faucet. Moreover I registered my pale and gaunt face in the mirror. I grieved with great lament and deliberation frightened by my own expression.

The next day in the glorious sunlight, with the wind of rage blowing in, I studied the fundament of my travails. With fond memory I combed through the past that led to an examination of my life. There I found that the magnetism of love and love's direction took place in a grand way. But that genuine love was long ago and far away. It seemed that this metamorphosis of my goal, object, and ambition in life had taken place when I was this young man. I was taking a blizzards course, both blind and deaf, but my courage was plentiful. And so I dashed away from the orchards in which I found myself toward the escarpment by the sea. There I drummed away at my unseen opponents, pondering my fate all the while. I was poised and radiant with keen and lucid

markings between myself and those of my comradery and foe.

In the hills of gentle slopes and greenness, under a blaze of sunshine, the water was running over the riverbed sweetly in chorus. Toward the sea the light flickered at the supine posture of the sun. Over the swells and brine it fell upon the spangled gulls on the sand and washed the entire shore as far as the eye could see. And so I used to linger upon this same edge of the world, fascinated by the ephemeral light.

From the beginning I struggled to make intelligible this 'vastness' of borders that had landed at my doorstep. It had bruised my confidence, to be sure, and I fell victim slowly and irreparably into their clutches uttering cries from deep within this darkness. Thus, invectives of effrontery and presumption introduced themselves. To hinder their impedance I began to brag, unashamedly, about my nature and temperament, about my seemingly endless good fortune and promise. Yes, I would purposely chortle by the sea, thrusting forth to lunge and stab at my repartee. As jubilant as if it were the holidays I would lilt to and fro. In the splendid night I would snub my enemy into a corner with sufficient cause for tears. The curses of generations seemed to flow through my body but my body was lean with a magnificent frame and interested only in a troupe with the athleticism inside me. I was, at times, whittling the 'fantastic' to a bout with insomnia. At other times, I would settle for

159

the bone of a dog. There was no way of seeing the future although it begged to be interpreted. Hence, early on I tried my best at prognostications. But the business, my business, of telling my own future was, alas, ebbing away. Nevertheless, with a slight juggling act I would make manifest every illuminating direction from my early life to the present.

This machine in the boundless skies however complex is hell-bent on eliminating such quiet chapters to my memoranda. To wish good fortune upon the behalf of angels is the only way, with the patience of time, to boast together a solution and an explanation. But who were these people about me: doctors, lawyers, private investigators, police, F.B.I., A.C.L.U., and palm readers? However, why should I limit it to these players above? Yes, it was time to say it, once and for all.

EVERYBODY, EVERYWHERE, WE WERE ALL INVOLVED! The only justice to prove helpful, (and that was only at the beginning), were the relations with the consanguinity of my family and the generous oaths of my dearest friends. Through these associations I managed to sometimes aver a form of truce with my wicked nemesis.

I began to rap my knuckles upon the desk. Like the rhythms of a finger drum I broke the rare and silent surface. It only proved that I sorely needed convalescence from the public eye as I needed the partnership of a landscape for this composition. Of course, it was mine to insist upon some form of justice and then there was, again, the cunning of the absolute. But these remarks neither served my sympathy nor aroused my indignation. They were simply fleeting perceptions

designed to save face in this apposition of
the unknown.   As I opened the window
the thrum and murmur of nature presented
itself. I was becoming careless in my habits
and slothful in my appearance. Scampering
about with my ablutions I managed to take
a shave and put on fresh clothing. The cold
water opened wide my eyes and prepared
me for the night to come.   Both watchful
and on guard I was reaching my last resort
to lash out at the covert, the concealment,
the refuge which offered itself day in and
day out with no other reason but to conquer
me. I had previously been too reserved for
violence.   Had   things   changed   so
dramatically?   The noise and sulfurous
bidding of my enemy made it difficult to
think. How was I to muzzle these jibes? I
wondered.   I have tasted this season with
rancor and bitterness and drained it to the
dregs.   My symptoms from this heated

162

enemy were thickset and commonplace. To resolve the many issues I would have to seek the intelligence of the supernatural or of the divine. The struggle of life by these measures has me tired and my attention was slowly becoming heedless toward any dubious result underfoot. My deliverance from these barbs was predicated upon a silence which had forsaken me. Pounding my feet to these troublesome cries was all that I could do and nothing more!

Within the dome of the heavens, between the ravenous sea and infinity, lay the glistening stars. There was nothing more or less this past week but a fury of insults. Was I to favor their methods and left-handed comments? To survive this exceeded the light of all myths and legends. I think to myself, what author said that it was better to suffer than to die? Understandably, I have lived these words and I don't choose to expire!

And so it was that I picked myself up from the floor and followed, again, the path to town. Whistling to banish thoughts of hunger I reviewed from memory the menu from last week. My emptiness had me writhing but paradoxically my spirits began to rise. After all, I was a part of the human race, damn it! There was no telling what flattery, what excessive flattery, lay at the end of the road. I am certain that many a traveler had lost sleep over my trials and tribulations. Why I wouldn't be surprised if many of these do-gooders had a place for me to eat, bathe, and rest once I was in the clear, so to speak. Whatever forces were at work there was persuasive evidence that, both philanthropy and misanthropy, were the warring factions. These ill-natured brutes propagated spleen and were not exceeded in number and intellect. Believe me their intelligence transcended my wildest expectations and I was first to salute them in their masterful game.

Even though this entire affair was clouded with gloom there was confirmation today that all was well no matter how far I had been driven by these bullies and lordly others. Yes, though I was tired and hungry my mind still spun like a top! Evidence of these outsiders doing good work, laboring over my safety and welfare, well, I was almost reduced to tears. These super telecommunications through sound, through electricity, and by laser were insurmountable means heralded by spirit-rapping, telekinesis, thought transference, and telepathy. Though not practiced in these fields of inquiry I was, nonetheless, stunned by their scrutiny, exhaustive analysis, and calculations matched by no others before. My closest secrets, the confidential 'kept under one's hat,' was as obvious to both these parties as a desert moon.

At the restaurant I felt at one with the human race. Though there were many patrons and a long wait I was at my best behavior. The affinity I had hoped for this very afternoon presently surrounded me. I checked into the reception room and then made haste to the bar. No sooner had I placed the order for my drink when, apropos of nothing, communications commenced. Instead of voices demeaning and bitter the do-gooders were at their best speaking very confidentially to me. In fact, there was a lilt and charm to these interlocutors as though we were old and intimate friends. Such as it should be, I declared to myself. And just then a woman beautiful and gracious showed me her smile, with laughter in her eyes.

Henceforth, I chuckled to my good-natured friends putting them at ease with a few happy and humorous thoughts. Good mirth was overwhelming and long overdue and I welcomed it with some contentment. It was so very simple. All that I had to do was to think with intentional and dramatically great enunciation and immediately my thoughts would be transmitted to its recipient.

The proximity to these good people was good to my soul but was, in fact, a double-edged sword. I chose to beam with delight at my own omniscience exposed by this high technology. The only equation I was not privy to was that of my chief complaint, that of robbing me of my livelihood and peace of mind with this assemblage of good and evil. I am certain that everyone had a skeleton or two in their closet. Wouldn't they all agree? This gradual exfoliation of my mind held to my eyes and those of others was truly a vice no human should have control over. How would anyone deal with this fortune telling, this divination? Look around you! Always there is someone by your side or within your grasp. Precisely, there is no place, secular or celestial, to seek neutrality or harmony of sorts. Listen to me. There is no place! We have been robbed of our time with serene contemplation and nature's peace. We have become victims of our inventions.

I know that fate has sealed a covenant of reward to pay for such a big prize. However, toward these thieves of the mind, well, I no longer trust anyone. There is such caprice. For now, you see, I can hear 'evil' pounding out its agenda to plunder the core and life of me. There is no longer the woman with laughter in her eyes nor anybody saluting me with good cheer. Perhaps I shall take another walk to the shoreline. I am immediately reminded of a poem once read. Something to do with the sound of waves drawing back and flinging pebbles thus bringing the eternal note of sadness in. Soon matters were resolving themselves, thank goodness. I

was no longer engaged in mischief. My heart was becoming lighter. These thugs and sluggards were no longer bent on humiliating me and nothing else. Twelve years of this ill collaboration of sorts. Twelve years, one for each apostle. I am hanging by a thread. Still timid, still lonely, I roam. I am still quite capable of summoning a feeling of irony and good humor but that will not bail me out. Ah, but something cried out from within me, 'was the entire city a legion of lunatics!' Henceforth I traveled toward home cursing everyone for their insolent role in my affairs. Approaching my destination I slowed down to recover my wits and to, once again, count my lucky stars.

The next morning I awoke from the boon of sleep. Wondering, of course, if the same game was being played outside I hastily showered and left for the haunt of my local café. Surely enough there were plain clothed sentries all about me and so, as before, I nodded to them conspiratorially. My solitude was beginning to hold me in constant retreat, always fearing for my life. Conversation was limited not just for myself but rather for my entourage as well! It was an obstacle and this perverse taciturnity had been practiced interminably. If there was something more physical, more palpable to this brotherhood, but instead there was only disagreement and blind ambitions. I would be obliging to take up arms for those watching out for me. I am certain that they would find the harvest of a fine mind with an accommodating temperament. However, they choose to whip me into servility rather than setting me on the right path. This was their fundamental blunder and it wasn't without repercussions.

In concert with a subdued calm I softly hummed as I walked away from this labyrinth of voices. I began to tremble from restraint and to long for the cliffs by the sea where I could shout out my bliss at the summit of the world. There I began to think about my last visit with a doctor and how he had avoided any diagnosis. Of course I didn't reveal any of these so-called symptoms to my illness as I knew very well that he himself was privy to the same signs. Could any such desperate sickness betray nature? I was, after all, familiar with voices and schizophrenia but I wasn't to be duped into believing I was capable of such madness and such magnitude. In fact, for a moment, a brief moment there was nothing extraordinary at my side. Nothing more than the breakers at the shore. Later I entered my house of lodging through the courtyard of wild flowers and ice plant. Locking myself inside I passed the kitchenette and threw myself upon the bed. Outside my window waved the greenery and flowers. To be mine thus far was more than trial and egregious error. But my patience had saved me more than once and I owed my life to it.

I hadn't worked for some time and I was almost penniless. It was not well planned but I decided to leave. My rent was up. I quickly sped off to the beach knowing it would have both a place for me to sleep and to shower. I could begin to see myself as a hermit. Once again I could only brood. But to hell with appearances, I moaned. With this sophisticated technology there was no escape! This was my one certainty, but a certainty I refused to accept. Still I subsisted in this gallery of faces where I craved to take into confidence someone without crude manners, a tender soul, someone not so despotic as this technology with whom to discuss matters, even if they appear petty.

Nonetheless, in this blue and naked day comes promise. Momentarily, my worries cease. This despair comes and goes as destiny dictates but, unfortunately, matters are out of my hands. I am simply antiquated man, walking upright and swinging his arms. But surely we must be able to arrive at some compromising and sensible solution! Hastening along the streets from a brief shower my misfortunes were mounting and I returned to my new home, a sandy knoll. In fact, my equilibrium was slipping and beginning to desert me altogether. Moreover, I could not help but immerse myself blinded by the injustice being served. For no rhyme or reason I stated my case. I spoke, or shall I say, whispered giving a fine performance at every pause. The fates that followed me wished only to pounce upon the graveyard of my ideas. Particularly, at night time the arcane nearly revealed their identity. At such times I would listen with rapt attention, preying on each and every sound. Sometimes solace grew until I would weep. Often I would saunter happily under the bridge where there lay the estuary from which I would luxuriate. Sometimes, without notice, I would strike out into the air. My design was to expunge these demons coughing and chattering at my side. There is no way to explain it but, from this acoustical bondage, somewhere along the lines I grew up. Still noise, articulate and inarticulate, makes one sometimes thrill and other times brood. At an especial interlude, in the soft murmur and rustle, I rub my temples to the stoned and broad silence. I realize that I must venture some place to disinter these 'sirens,' to up end them, one by one, like blocks or ice floes into the sea.

I take a brisk swim and I dry myself off. Again I ask, why am I an exception? What am I guilty of? I do not wish to conceal myself anymore than the next fellow. I long to get to the bottom of these loathsome inquiries. However, straight down into the depths of my mind I have been ransacked. There is nothing left to think or to be. Nothing! What of this despotism that insists upon my guilt? Was I merely guilty of a petty crime or the subject of an experiment? With this abundant secrecy I sincerely doubt the former but not the latter. But I must confess that many queer things and convoluted reasoning do abide everywhere. Why had I, one day, been unearthed from my simple, domestic life? This evil faction had become irritable for no reason. But that was only in the beginning. Presently, relations have become much more strained as threats sounding from everywhere engulf me. Why do these devils insist upon my guilt? Why are we incompatible? Why am I treated with such a diet of crudities, such undisguised contempt? I desperately need to take into confidence anyone with ears to hear of my complaints without biased presupposition or surly judgment. A mere stranger? Why of course! (Though there were no 'true' strangers, only players!)

Furthermore the vigor of my mind, together with this insomnia revisiting me, makes for a dubious hash, a feverish mind with peevish sensibilities. However, it wasn't up to me to champion such a predicament. I must shout 'for crying out loud, why had they chosen me?' What were their intentions, rifling my mind without cessation? What disguises should I don? What masks should I assume? Where shall I take my elopement?

I have been chased off to this embankment of sand in good time and measure and soon I would find myself a complete nomad. Nevertheless this was not so disagreeable as this period in my life demanded more freedom and less responsibility. Yes, feasting on the brotherhood of the outdoors was, perhaps, how to die happy! Is there any other question?

Some solace was forthcoming. Oh, to be sure! But I can no longer think clearly. At this juncture I no longer care much about the secret methods that they employ. I have become a tramp and weary traveler. It is, after all, man's inhumanity to man that I suffer and for such grief there is no cure. Those who surround me seem eminently vulgar and incurious as custom dictates. Even though, at times, I feel death near I am happily surprised at my strength, my Olympian strength. 'May we all go, not quietly into the night!'

II

This morning I was getting along quite well from the very start. Though it seemed as though there were human jackals at every turn of the road I naturally found myself acting the part of the fool to stave off their madness. I must say that though there were these numberless cheats and swindlers there was likewise the torchlight of the common man at every significant post. In fact, one good soul had left a ten dollar bill beneath my pillow as I slept. And so I decided to treat myself to a small meal after stowing away my gear.

My hostess walked me to my seat. Both of us smiled knowing, good and well, what our functions were. Being in the center of things made me feel a little uncomfortable and I was happy when my waitress arrived.

Now I had on a long face as everyone seemed to eye me. With the length of time that had elapsed between my last social event and today I was rummaging through memory and feeling faint despair on my face. It had been ages ago, not worth the

179

telling, since I had visited this type of place. It surprised me how immense was the courage one needed to dine alone. But after some time I lifted my head. When I thanked her for my coffee she seemed to blush. My reply was too profuse, I thought, and I began to contemplate my own nature. It was the nature of a man driven to his knees and plausibly endangering those around him. Never was I far away from this burdensome introspection and I upbraided myself for any unbecoming behavior. I was dressed rather shabbily, it should be noted, and yet I wasn't irreproachable. It was entirely up to me to clutch the dogma of fine manners as objectionable or excessive as they might seem. In light of this tiresome parade of faces I should guide myself as tastefully as possible not letting go of any of the countless secrets at my disposal. Yes, I was

180

a celebrity of sorts and it would do me no good to drive deeper into the clefts of reasonable argument. To seize my demeanor and disperse it with consummate skill was my task and my irrepressible impulse. Many times this had saved me from the pits of hell.

Ah, but there is time before I am crushed! All I can do is all a man could do, I told myself, and that is to search for new beginnings. I must succeed in summoning a display of sound judgment, making friends all the while. However, with nothing to busy my mind I felt, at once, a debt was owed on my behalf. I experienced, how do you say, an obligation to prune and shear my composition such that any devotee that was to read the manuscript would see clearly enough the great wager of my patience in the rough copy or draft. In short, I wasn't going out without a fight! Yes, 'try and try again,' was my motto. Such an edict has me pacing but not retreating. It has promise but not yet the marrow that evolves from such creations. Come hell or high water I would make of myself the centerpiece right down to the final gallery proof. No, I was not at the end of my rope. I wouldn't surrender my post. But how long before I walked, hand in hand, with injustice? How long must I dwell in the pall of my nemesis? Questions but, again, no answers! My final departure begged for a decisive conclusion. For example, the benevolent would have to be abundantly praised with copious tears. Secondly, I would have to chronicle this poor and disreputable history of myself, the drifter. I promise myself that if I lift myself up to the heavens with verse, the sky will be filled with splendor. But for now I don a Panama hat and bear the fierce sunlight on the flux of the sea.

I have been imprisoned now for years but without a scratch. It isn't the darkness but the cold that I fear. The boughs of the trees sway like sails. I am an average man reclining toward the stars. Here my heart quickens in its sovereignty. But I am left to cringe from the irresolute. I am left to chronicle these ragged but living memoirs. No matter how difficult I must employ my deepest resources and strike out like the warrior they have made of me. If I was a hunchback the public would point at my ugliness and deformity. But my present mental stature insists that I go unnoticed no matter what the crimes are against me. No such deformity is leveled against me no matter how grotesque the circumstances.

I would like to throttle both good and evil alike. After all, they had bifurcated from the same root. But it is the hush of night. The darkness has crept in to claim me. I am all alone. In this great solitude I assume the posture of a tramp. Here I wait for the reluctant public to encircle me, hand in hand. Here I wait to put a glorious seal on the doings of these actors beside me. And here I will wait, and wait, and wait until death do us part!

The wind changes, the rumors cease. However, mine is not to despair over such trifles and these supernumerary impressions. I have presently been assured of olfactory hallucinations to add to these visual, auditory, and tactile ones. My nose was gathering new datum, flooding my senses with old memorabilia. Now I inhabit the vestibules above hell where my troubles end in exhaustion. Nature has come apart and still it summons me. Moreover, to ape these beginnings of a new book I shall engage these wanderers, trolling in waters fathoms deep. Toward this end I have pledged to reel with efforts beyond measure. This morning, at the bay, I was privy to the long and low sadness of the foghorns, the trudging of the barges, the push into the sink, and the cold mist like a supernatural fog. Sometimes this weighed upon me while at other times it filled me with wonder.

To remedy my wounds I began to ask people the time of day. At least it was a start, I thought. And I continued on in this same vein, punctuating my casual stroll with these annoying ploys to arouse people's attention. Hadn't they, more than once, more than scores of times put it into my head that I was a writer worthy of gifts? Along these lines I told the poor man beside me, "I beg your pardon, sir, I am not a narcissist!" He began to reply and then shook me off as if I was a fly. Well, I didn't want to get chummy with the likes of him and I said as much. Trotting away I called to him with savage and bloodthirsty cries. In so doing I scared the daylights out of not only him but myself as well.

I decided that it was time to snooze and I pedaled my way to the park. Lying in the grass I took in the inhabitants by my side. Complete calm enveloped me as opposed to my earlier rage and I could feel my eyes close to the mellow sun. Awakening I found myself uncommonly clear sighted, effervescent with ideas and drama. Others had come before me and their message was clear-persevere, they tell me, persevere! Yes, my only duty was not to suppress that which lay within. I must be as playful and docile as a puppy. In the streets that I walk there is disillusionment in the air. I will not supervene with dull wit but I will ask these impostors to

occasionally let us sing and shout to our heart's content. I began to jot down notes, notes that abound with good sense among this turmoil. I was more and more proud of these words that flew by me. Effortlessly I scribbled despite my nemesis. The workings of my mind were superb. One word, then the next, I put down for posterity, unable to focus upon any special theme. But what did that matter to me for I was onto something and I would not be silenced by such phobias and good manners. Nobody could refuse these words. They were ensconced in gold and ready for the printing press. However, I realized, there was more than just pleasing myself. I must make it palatable to the public. Oh, but the words are flying as of flint and the fires are burning. As of lightening they will strike. I am finally out of dope for these consolations. In fact there are such little snippets left now at this calling and I will, without a doubt, renounce them one by one.

This went on for weeks until I could finally brook no more. I wasn't any longer going to play the wind up toy. It was the middle of the night when I awoke with a start. All of this humbuggery had me on edge. Looking on without any emotion wasn't my style. As such I packed up my belongings and humped it down to an all night café. On my way I grimaced, uttering malign thoughts. Before entering I noticed cigarette ends and paper trash. It was just my luck that there were a half dozen policeman eating together. They had their nerve, I thought. I nearly cried out 'there is strength in numbers' but I let it go and nrvously fidgeted with the utensils. I could swear that one of them winked at me but I couldn't be sure. Whatever and whoever was trailing me was still a mystery and it was running me ragged. One thing for certain there was no dearth of players in this enigma. Like it or not I was a marked man!

Over my coffee I was almost sniffling, shyly weeping but with resolution. What must I do but to shake the sense from these ghouls? It was quite clear that madness lay no claim to me. No, at this I was an unfaltering pugilist, fighting day and night. It wasn't a mission for the faint-hearted.

The coffee was beginning to pick me up. I no longer scowled at the police and I left them to their own brand of surveillance. The waitress was kind enough to pour me one coffee after the other. Her voice was hoarse but her manners sublime. I was beginning to feel exalted. She didn't speak much and I wasn't going to be importune with solicitations. One of the policeman's eyes were fixed upon me as if I was a common criminal. Perhaps he was interested in my person watching me, as he was, with great curiosity. He doubtless knew of the many miles I had traveled. Did he expect me to fall out of character, to crouch and to strike? With what distortion was he attributing to me? I was far beyond railing with him or anyone else. For one thing to wrangle as such I would have to possess the energy that I was lacking. For now, what with the geniality of the waitress, I was feeling quite tender. 'That's the spirit' I told myself. Still the absurdity of this chase had me coming and going. How was I to right the wrong? What would prove to be my redemption? If they had me

in such fetters why would they shy away
from disguising me and relocating me away
from these devils? Why had they clung to
me this past year? Why had I so easily put
trust in these matters? Why had I written so
much? A word, any word, would set me
off, inspiration or not. And the maxims that
issued from my lips were sometimes
staggering. Why had I ravished the
language so seeking publication if it were
not for some form of legitimacy and
retribution? Of this world, of this miner's
gold I was determined to prop myself up.
Shedding tears for words I sometimes
succumb to the dear look of other's eyes. At
times I was the mouthpiece of serenity and
at other times the rage of fire. But I was
ultimately servile to humanity. As
perpetual as the seasons yet as ponderous
with grief. Often without satisfaction I was

faced with these rivals without equal. If only I could sit this one out. If only I could take a well deserved respite from these elements of vigil. What of ignorance had I partaken? Where lay the truth to my observations and profound efforts? Of what improprieties had I been guilty? In my dreams I am sometimes so barbarous. How would I best serve my time, occupying myself with substance and divesting myself of the disjecta membra?

But it is a fine day and I am miles ahead of myself. The custodian is mopping the floor of the café with a jigging motion. It smells as if it was ether. For a moment I put my head down willing to die if it was meant to be so. Then I rebound back to the living world making haste to the door. The demons running this show have gone so far as to put a man, a vagrant to boot like myself, poised upon the patio to break the ice. But I am now as tired as the day is long and I pass him without incidence. No need to pout about the trouble that I have somehow gotten myself into. I am simply a man among men and I had bought myself another hour.

I took the long road back to the city from this rural café. I hadn't checked my mail at the post office for a few days now and I was getting myself worked up over any replies to my literary mailings. I mumbled some strange incantations, then I opened the mailbox. There before my eyes lay the returned envelop to one of my manuscripts. I tore it open as fast as I could and I caught my breath. Suddenly the unthinkable was presented to me. 'Congratulations' it read. My story had been accepted and there was a handsome piece of change with the accolades given me. 'An expert piece of work' it said. I nearly burst into tears it being such a lovely and unexpected bit of news. It couldn't have come at a better time. I was dreadfully tired of sleeping in the brush with only pennies to procure my bread. Henceforth I steeled away to a boarding house bent on renting a room day by day.

An elderly woman filled with contempt for such vagrants as myself reluctantly showed me a room. Brimming with hope I revealed to her my letter of acceptance. No, I was no ordinary vagrant. I was a writer and a damned good one. I let her know without pause that I was no troublemaker. She seemed to accept my line of reasoning and soon I was installed taking a long, hot shower and laying down to rest from the lack of sleep this prior night.

Awakening some few hours later I marched downtown almost shouting with joy. No other harbinger of good will passed by me left or right. Instead, there was solemnity in the air as if my acceptance of this short story had somehow annoyed them.

It was time, once again, to visit another barber. There I fell into conversation with an older gentleman who had been cutting hair for fifty years. The talk was of trifles but endearing as I hadn't spoken but briefly to anyone in months. I nearly asked him if I could be of any help sweeping up and cleaning the shop but I declined not wishing to sully this friendship of sorts nor to reveal my meager finances. I figured that I owed him already for being so frank with me and so generous with conversation. In fact I felt some sorrow and pity for him what with the nervous tic in his left eye. He also seemed to balance himself on one foot, then the other, as if he was a child and had to urinate. As for me I began to tell him of my literary exploits sparing no conceit over my latest acceptance of a short story and my present project of a novella. He seemed intrigued yet questionable about my endeavors; the nature, that is, of my vocation and his mistrust for it. He seemed to have read only one page of Freud and he was quick in quoting one of his favorite passages. "Anxiety harbors a wish." By the end of our conversation I was developing a tic in my eye as well and I couldn't wait to dash out of sight.

Enough, I said to myself, enough! I was beginning to feel like an outcast from his words and I made a pledge not to return here in the future. He, no doubt, held some high post and in this volley of our chat was duping me for my entourage. As I departed I told him quite succinctly that I figured that he was a mathematician, tongue in cheek, one who gambled the ponies, I smirked. Then I stormed out glad to see the sunlight once again.

My moods were presently passing as light and shadow. Had I lain down to wrangle with this barber and how far had they gotten to me? My mood had swung around. Was I being put out to pasture with the likes of him, the barber? The further that I examined it the greater it seemed to me that he had tricked me, deceived me into believing in himself rather than me. Well, I'll be damned, I thought, if I should divest my integrity for his parasol of words. Henceforth I began to rant and to rave at this impostor. He had me so worked up that I felt sheer buoyancy in pounding out my novella. No, I wouldn't accept the likes of him addressing myself as some insignificant stooge. He was out of character for his part and this much was certain. These rivals, these infamous others had supervened my chatter about myself and I wasn't feeling pleased about it.

Despite the words of the barber the day has been glorious. I tramp back home to my old Victorian and I will write at breakneck speed. My words are palatable and effortless. They are coming forth as savory as a good meal. I have to urinate but I can't break off with my writing. I began to stagger a little facing this biological need and I put down my pen to relief myself. Sure enough when I return the tap has run dry. I reread the last lines and I am pleased.

But I will have to take a walk to restart my engine. And so to the library I traipse committed to more inventions. There I feel rage growing toward these 'good people' and I began to pound at the keys of the computer bent on exacting some type of revenge. I would show them all how the cow ate the cabbage! I would write another novella and become a respected author deserving the highest of honors. There would be no doubt nor contest to my stature and I would be well on my way to a successful career.

I continued typing, frothing at the mouth, until closing time. I took my valise and headed to the supermarket. There I bought bread and ham and headed home for this little repast but not before a smile from the counterperson. Apparently some of these people were still respectful of what

I had endured and I was quick to reply in kind. One couldn't hold a grudge against these other forsaken persons who had gotten on my bad side. Yes, we were pals, she and I, and there was no telling how far things might go. I lingered there until I could no longer keep silent. I would ask her out for a modest meal or coffee. To my surprise she responded favorably. It was settled! We would meet at the café down the street at four tomorrow afternoon. I departed my heart singing to this fine and sunny day.

But at home, crouched by the draperies in a cold sweat, I began feeling petrified by my intentions with this tryst. It would seem that the correct tact would be to introduce myself as the author I hadn't yet fully become. I must fill her head with my dreams regardless of the mendacity of tre terms. I must woo her in an incredible way never letting her know of my true past, of my homelessness, and my wayward ways. I was an author, damn it, and worthy of praise I repeated. Certainly I could make her see reason. Certainly there would be no doubt as to my authenticity. I must attack on all fronts not giving her the chance to reflect upon nor ponder my thoughts before I let go of the arrow. It must be done diplomatically but with some degree of conceit. The main thing was to deceive her with the gladness of a performing artist. There was no denying it I was a brave soul. Trudging through these matters with my head held high I would swing 'round to encompass the climes that be my witness to this forbidden fruit. Oh, but my heart is already broken and I haven't yet met with this poor soul of my dreams. I must, and this is imperative, catch her before she falls for my rhetoric.   We met at the café. She looked even more winsome than before and this derailed me. I was being seduced by the charms of her gaze. I must confess I was a little unnerved. If those trailing me were to think us conspirators they might, very well, follow her causing the same pangs that had been delivered to me. On the other hand if she was a part of those guilty in watching over me she might know all about me and my lies would be manifest. As a result of these considerations flying by me I attempted to drive a wedge between her true identity and a false one adopted to deceive me. If she was innocent I would no longer trample upon her feelings. Quite the contrary. I would worry for her safety and summon a fraternal attitude absolving her of the crime of knowing me and thus rescuing her from evil. Perhaps we would even feign an argument for those watching us. It would be a quarrel that would portray an act of impatience and repulsion with one another. Verging on the loathsome we would astonish all and sundry and later, at a safer time, we would fall prostrate with laughter thinking about this invented scene at the café. But would we be able to transcend the sophistication of their technology and fool them altogether or would they call our bluff? It must be said that though I never directly met the men and women espying me I was sound of mind and certain of their presence. I knew from experience that they wouldn't be able to crush my spirits even if at times their snobbery and insults wounded me.

As for my writing ambitions who would be my audience? Was I ignoble in my language? Was I being systematically shattered? A man my age in such condition as was I, well, it was deplorable. The lies never stopped and was it my imagination or was she scowling at me? More than ever I longed for a soul mate, one that would bequeath to me peace of mind. For now I can write to my heart's content and be no closer to complete satisfaction with my life. Inside myself I must put all of these attendants to the test. Me and my unseemly coat and my austere and rigid image would never say 'give.' At other times listen to me purr. Yes, I had a soft side to this character and occasionally I was bent over with laughter even though I didn't always know why. Typically patience was my dear friend and only seldom was there a savage turn of events. At still other times I was sullen and I would sob at the dim prospects of things. Here the forces that be would serve me from getting too worked up over matters that were out of my control.

But presently our discussion was leaning toward the finish and, at once, I drew myself back from any more meditations on my part. I thanked her profusely for her company and let it go at that. The bells of the elevator and the screeching of the sliding door found us on the pavement where there ensued a silence that I had never known. To break the monotony I made casual references to the finery of her dress, intoning warmly that I hadn't had such an assignation in many long months. (Though it had been longer than this I didn't wish to appear too terribly desperate.) As we parted I walked rapidly, babbling like a fool, cursing myself for my deceit and buckram. What ugliness had possessed me among this crowd that wouldn't release me?

In this regard I prayed for her safety against the vulgarity of these ghouls and I made tracks home. The long and short of it was that we had collaborative thinking and I had concurred that she was a friend, not foe. No, she wasn't my nemesis by any means and if she was she had transcended my acting ability altogether. Yes, I was playing the part of the romantic and I slapped myself on the back for the courage it took to not only ask her out but to converse very lively through the quagmire of my life. The nasty bit of news was that I would have to skip a few meals to make up for the expense of the coffee house. Though I was committed to seeing her again I couldn't very well afford it nor disclose my financial status. Anyway, time would tell and besides I was buzzing with new and fresh ideas for my novel. Disengaged from my errant wanderings I scrambled home but not without an insolent greeting from the manager on the stoop. Nonetheless, I was 'home' again and I soon took to writing. Would I prevail? But of course! For my mood had swung around and I wasn't about to hear any more discouragement, even though looking down at the garden I was reminded of this loathsome creature, Ruth. Skulking no more I was astonished at my creative output driving all of these alien forces away and all of the litter of the evening while walking home. At the behest of my conscience I strove to put an end to any belittling thoughts. I pampered the words and made them as palatable and newsworthy as possible. For instance, if a

207

character had a bum leg I would see to it that he limped with just the proper labor and his face would reveal his suffering. Yes, as if he was the only cripple that we all had known. If he was schizophrenic he would shout at the top of his voice to everyone and to nobody. To curtail his suffering he would gesticulate wildly, blubbering with song, and banishing evil spirits along his way. He would bashfully beg citing inanities and foolishness with the drop of a hat. He would be the man on the street or crouched behind shrubbery, underfed and without warm clothing during the winter. He would be the man we all know walking tirelessly and ranting to beat the devil. On the cusp of insanity he would hobble merrily along using unseemly language with which to trample these undeserving others. He would be the

first and last man falling and he would do
this all for honor and posterity! Intuition
would be his master and there would be no
other before him. He would succor the sun
and the stars and avoid the encroaching
darkness while summoning a hurrah for
this philosophy of light.

III

It is settled! Today I will take a walk
the likes of which I have never tramped.
The flowers and the birds will come
knocking as will the trees and the sky. It
will be a glorious day, one made for song. I
wouldn't sink so low as to eschew these
advances of nature. I will remain upright.
Words, like feathers, will alight upon my
shoulders. I will promote myself and my

writing but this inwardness must cease. My mind is a broken clock and the 'eternal now' has set in. This cunning that cuts me to the quick is a stones throw from the alluvium of great trespasses. Meanwhile I have taken a long look at my life, at the attributes that precede me. The thrill is no more when we shall meet. Things have all gone up in smoke and there is no respite from these struggles. I must coddle these words of mine for I am finding that they are extremely tender. While it is true that I am a novice to writing I am, nevertheless, presently surprised at these proceedings between myself and the publishers. But why I sometimes exalt they merely frown.

Thankfully this is rare. For such a long time there had been an impasse which I couldn't transcen. But today is my day of reckoning. Today I find that I have had another manuscript published. My ecstasy is

well deserved. For such a long
time I was the only one to believe in my
talent and I thought that I should go mad if
something wasn't done about it and soon!
For crying out loud, I almost shouted! Even
with my imperfections I was reeling. The
virulent and bitter attacks from other
prospective publishers have vanished. No
longer was I an outsider selling snake oil.
About their objectionable replies I hadn't
cowered. In the distance I could hear songs
of old but I am without nostalgia. Tonight I
will sleep the sleep of the dead, without
remorse, without any encumbrance of mind
or body. With my writing I have gambled
and it is paying off. But was I to jump from
some height or swim far out to sea. 'They'
were all beckoning me with nothing left to
spare. Still good fortune rains down upon
me. Tongue in cheek I wouldn't let them

down without breaking their hearts, poor darlings. The public, it appears, is coming to see their writer. Let me be hung by my heels. What I have wished for and what has been granted is colossal and I won't expect less. Night and day I have worked it, humped it for what it was worth. Though I am engaged to my books I sometimes hate them with a fury. It is, at times, a match made in hell but I have to abide by it. Soon 'they' will come for me despite my publications. I have no idea why but I shall hang my head and go silently. It is my way and it always has been. When confronted by opposition I always recoil even though I am inclined to deny this with false bravado. But it is in the late hours now and sheer fatigue is setting in. I have no doubt that future proceedings will see me through. I agree that I shall surrender but not grovel. I will give them my name only never forgetting my origins of strength. My demureness will have 'them' coming and going and there shall be nothing to follow me down these long and sad corridors to my little room.

What is more I will be flowered with a reprieve and take my lunch with others in my same condition. When my mind is depleted with their interrogations I will return to accept my prize for writing. No matter how merciless is their probe I will educt some obscure pleasure from their wanderings. I will not only be invincible but will attain some form of bliss with which to seize these others and their egregious actions. If I become lost, simply lost, I will return to my roots and no longer be forsaken.

But I am beginning to rant like a

madman, I suppose, and my hunger is dictating my agenda. Soon those around me would, perhaps, recognize me and my post as an author. Yes, it was a form of stardom and stardust and to top it off I would no longer be left in the cold with my blanket and thermos of coffee. But my moods are now fading in then out and I am losing my grasp of the situation. So before eating I decided upon a plan to visit the grocery clerk and to apprize her of my latest publication. I was glistening now, frothing at the mouth to watch her expression at my good and great news. Perhaps I had told her one too many lies for she seemed to deter me with her eyes, almost shunning me away. I quickly dismissed myself muttering, under my breath, 'to the devil with you.' But even with this disappointment I was not used up quite yet.

I would not permit her contempt for me spoil my good fortune. Besides I was bound to win the hearts of many others who would esteem me for my gifts and my good name, I might add. Yes, 'son,' I told myself, you are in for the time of your life. There is no telling how bright your future shall be and I began to thumb my nose at these fine upstarts among me. Pistols or swords, ladies and gentlemen, and I chuckled to myself all the way to a fine restaurant. It was a restaurant whose menu I had espied in the window days earlier but without entering.

A party of one, I snickered. However, the hostess was in no mood for conversation and I was forced to retreat within to avoid her scowl. What was a fine day to me was not, it was plain to see, true for others. So be it, I thought to myself. I will toast to myself and refuse them the opportunity to belittle me and disparage my good news. Things were going smoothly but when it appeared that others were mocking me I gave up on this attempt at merriment polishing off my food and avoiding all eyes penetrating me. Why was it necessary for them to make of me an object of ridicule wasting my time and good graces? Thus I departed without the slightest gratuity.

At home I lounged, reading my letter of acceptance over and over again. I was becoming quite infatuated with myself and my prize. My mind was corpulent with their laudable words and I didn't let one word go by unnoticed. I savored their terms with the ambitions of a novice making, perhaps, a bigger thing out of it than was meant to be. Nonetheless, there lay the words in the greatest of splendor readily absorbed into my entertaining mind. I began to toy with the ideas of a new book, one far superior to the one accepted by this publishing house. It would entail plenty of ground work but it was, indeed, quite possible that I had something by its tail. And so, swept away by these considerations, I began to pen fresh missives inspired by this dear letter. One word after another came my way without refrain. Far from resting upon my laurels I jabbed and jotted down an outline that was commendable by any standards. I was having a time of it, my head swimming with new matter, new songs, and savory exploits. It was the writer's life and it appealed to each and every sense. However, noise rang out down the hall. I merely responded by telling them 'all' that they couldn't keep a good man down. But after a while this annoyance began to intrude into my affairs. As a result I turned on a fan to drown out some of the racket. However, Ruth fortunately intervened and I was spared this bother for the time being. My fate was presently being written beneath the sun and I was being crowned with glory. Should there be any other disturbances I would take to the streets to remedy this scourge. But was it time to quit or was I just beginning? I could sense the whispers as soft as baby's breath and it summoned me but without peril. But deep down what of my own amorphous cry shall be heard?

The next day I was unaccustomedly light hearted. It had been arranged that I hasten by train to the publishing house. There was much to be done in little time.

The signing of papers as well as a rigorous editing of the book was in order. Fortunately the publisher would furnish me with living quarters for the time being.

The sky was glittering with the wings of birds. It had been a long, long while since I had been out of town and the anxiety of travel was digging into me. It would be approximately two hours travel time before the train arrived at my destination and I lunched on a sandwich to keep up my strength. I peered at the text of my book with great pride making points of analysis here and there. Though at times I was a little disconcerted at my prose it, nevertheless, held water and I was excited to find the eyes of my editor and publisher to improve my book.

My editor, Ray, picked me up at the train depot. I had so long been in solitude honing my craft alone that there was extreme pleasure in having allies and I let them know this when introductions took place. In fact my isolation had been so complete that the joyful contrast found me with tears in my eyes. All the while, I must admit, there were reservations about not only my safety but the safety of others as well. If my allies and nemesis were close by who knows what evils were immanent. It surprised me that I was being permitted to publish a book as my words often told about a set of very secretive circumstances. However, the presence of my new found friends comforted me to no end and I discovered myself to be in good company with each passing day. Never in years had I passed the time with others so fondly and I began to entertain the notion that I should relocate here for both convenience and to quiet my fears. Yes, such solace was entirely opposed to my former address and the more I thought about it the more intimate I became with these newborn reflections. I proposed this bit of news to Ray and almost like family he heartedly agreed. And so on my last day we went by car to a number of boarding houses and apartments.

I had been given legitimacy and a new career and this propped me up against both reasonable and unreasonable fears. No longer, it appeared, would homelessness supervene upon my livelihood. In this regard I was making leaps and bounds from my former life. Yes, I had gambled with my writing and it had paid off! Now I found my pockets were being lined with gold and new friends were being made. My dreams had been answered and I had fallen in love with my vocation. But despite this love there was still lingering questions. There was still some reluctance and slight regret about my acceptance of these terms. No doubt they stemmed from this secret society that still abound around me. But hell, I thought, if they could do no more than follow me why should I be annoyed. Our journey to different housing had been successful. I found a studio that was perched above a canyon of trees and birds, a place that would be ideal for living and creating. With an advance to my salary I put money down to secure my new dwelling. Then I whistled a merry tune as we left for the train station. Never in years had I felt so free from danger nor so invulnerable with my surroundings and I couldn't wait to install myself in my new flat.

The radiant bloom of the flowers at my new haunt bourgeoned about me and I remained quite calm and possessed with my good fortune. No longer would I have to tolerate the mean-spiritedness and derision of Ruth and most of the inhabitants of the town. In fact there wasn't a soul with whom to say farewell. I had become eminently alone there and almost met with a bad turn of fate more than once. The entire reticulum of the streets I had walked so many times hungry and without shelter lay before my eyes like a desperate dream. No amount of reverie nor appeasement abated my revulsion. My only dream now was to move on to my new home and friends. After thinking it over I decided not to tell Ruth about my move. No, why split hairs with the likes of her loathsome and disgusting manners. So I packed my one bag and my satchel. As my old one was quite worn out I had discovered a burlap sack with which to hoist my few belongings and I made good use of it. Then I walked downstairs to my freedom and my new life. Were some person or entity to confront me now with the confidential nature and enigma of my situation I would merely laugh in their faces. I took the long walk to the train depot filled with excitement and visions of my new life and I didn't once look back. I was reveling in anticipation. I felt like a celebrity gazing at a golden future and I felt myself laughing like a madman. I hadn't realized the stranglehold this town had on me until I contrasted it with my new home and success. Accordingly I shook my fists with rage at the harm 'they' nearly did to me.

Later I boarded the train and made

myself comfortable. I wanted to tell every one of my conquests and my happiness but instead I listened quite calmly at the departure being announced over the intercom and I finally broke, like a child, into tears.

Perched in my new home the prophecies are rushing in. No more dire sacrifices have been made as in the former town. Only gentle covenants exist between myself and Ray. Expressions, revelations, and divine utterances come my way softly, almost aromatically, when the lights are low. Nothing too excessive, nothing too elaborate, I draw the line and abide by it. Thus I have staked out a claim to my little fortune. There are no other games to play and without any misgivings I am inclined to thrive on it. All that remains was that 'she,' the woman of my dreams, lay in my arms with sweet kisses and undying love.

It is a long night in a torrential rain. I have changed addresses to denounce my former struggles and to seek out a love that will chase away any melancholy. For, you see, my sadness has reappeared without warning and I fear that with it will come ill health. However, with the friendships of my publisher and the working crew I was in good hands and we passed many splendid times toasting to our health. Predictions of more writing to come were being satisfied one day at a time and I couldn't remember when writing had been so facile. With candor I was treading on one composition after another. At times I seemed to be without rival though, at other moments, I lacked something of significance. Still things were generally quite rosy and I would often tip my hat to the creative forces that be for my deliverance.

The rain stopped and I decided upon a jaunt downtown. There was a park on the way where the birds were being fed and a large fountain spouted water. I sat down upon a bench with an elderly man and while feeding the pigeons he began to recite the story of his life. Without pause he elaborated upon his first and second wives who were now dead and about his two children and grandchildren. He stopped only once to ask me if I had any children but he didn't permit me to answer proceeding with haste his lengthy story in all its glory. After twenty minutes of this rant I finally could take no more. I quickly dismissed myself as he kept up with this banter with no end in sight. Feeling somewhat relieved I rushed to Ray's office to discuss my book.

He was pleased with my rough draft but told me to trim some of its excess. Showing me a few instances of this mistake I had to agree with his appraisal and I told him that sometimes 'flapdoodle' got in my way. He laughed out loud at this analogy but detecting my delicacy and sensibilities told me not to make much of it.

A new editor, a woman by the name of Charlotte, entered the room and we were introduced. She seemed dreadfully shy and I tried to put her at ease. Ray had a grand sense of humor and he had us rolling in the aisles over his jests. I discovered laughter that had been missing for such a long time as well as the good health that accompanied it. But soon it was time to get back to work and we all went our separate ways.

Back home with my lap top I chased down the excess that Ray had discovered and I began to operate. Incisively I cut and pruned the text trimming it of its repletion. His criticisms helped to make it sing and I was grateful for his commentary. I didn't know exactly why I hadn't espied such deficiencies and I made a mental note to avoid these same mistakes in the future. That night it dawned on me. With my minor skills at illustration I might very well pen some children's stories or fairy tales for the adult. It might be worth the while. Perhaps there would be a new niche for me. A smattering of talent would be all that it took, or so I guessed. But all of a sudden loneliness and sadness cut deeply and mercilessly into me. I was growing older alone. I began to hum to myself for company and to muse about the positive things in my life. For whatever reasons things turned abruptly and I began to count my lucky stars.

To write a fairy tale I found that I would have to give myself completely. Though it was, to some degree, a matter of simplicity I nevertheless discovered that it was far from the ease with which I had composed my novellas. The deeper that I dug though the more optimism shone my way. I was rediscovering my childhood largely with confidence and the sanguine. I was no longer mirroring so much of the despair in my life as my previous writings.

Soon I was the happy recipient of a children's story. The first one was to deal with a talking teapot. Here my imagination began to soar. Endearing pictures alighted upon my shoulders and I sketched them one by one. By nightfall I had written and roughed out drawings of my characters. What would Ray think of these inspirations? I wondered. The next morning, bright and early, I awoke and pedaled my wares to Ray. He was visibly impressed and he proposed a publisher of children's books. Things were looking up. No longer did dread come my way. To my surprise Ray handed to me a rather handsome royalties check and we both laughed over our success. He suggested that I draw the cover of my latest novel and I full heartedly agreed. What I would sketch I hadn't the faintest idea but my heart was in it and I couldn't be stopped by any mental blocks in the foreseeable future. The book had been written and almost shouted out at me for illustration. It would be a welcome surprise, that much was certain.

One week later I presented to Ray a dozen various drawings for print. He seemed to be decided upon one in particular and I happily conceded. He showered me with accolades to this last book and asked me if I had anymore in the offing. I told him that I had copious notes but that nothing was quite settled as of yet. He encouraged me in this direction but told me with some candor and persistence that my children's book might well be pursued for the meantime to pacify more serious work and to permit me a pause from its grueling content. I assented to these perceptions telling him that my fairy tale was nearly completed and that I looked forward to a resumption of my 'psychological' novels. In the meantime I would polish off what appeared to be a successful children's book. However, it would depend upon the publisher. I wasn't quite sure of their reaction it being my first book of this nature and, of course, there lay the fact that I never had children of m own.

It was a Tuesday and my confidence prevailed as I took my book to market. Sure enough they accepted it and it seemed that I could do no wrong in this game of writing. I was buoyant with joy and I told them as much. Hopefully, they mentioned, it would be available by Christmas. It was now time to return to my 'serious' books. Perhaps a sequel to my last novella. I poured through my handwritten notes drawing up an itinerary and outline of my novel to be. But while typing them on my lap top I noticed something as of company. The computer began talking to me in a hushed voice. I began to listen, cocking my head to and fro to get the most out of these mutterings. 'Who are you, what do you want,' I queried. Oh, but they vexed me not replying in kind

233

but instead rushing forth with their agenda. It was as though they were stalking me and bent on their own conclusions. I insisted that they answer me but they wouldn't cease with their banter. I felt like seizing these devils by the throat and hurling them through the window. They had shown me quite a blow and this mischievous clout had done its damage. I was afraid to go outside! Still I was curious if something out there, as well, was ridden with more machinations. And so I crept outside passing the gardenias and the shadows from the trees. Sure enough outside there was a landslide of abomination. They had me coming and going. If it weren't for the inborn reservations I held toward these adventurers I would have abdicated many times over. About these misfits, well, I neither found them charming nor that controlling yet. They were simply obstacles to overcome. I must wrap it up as I had before. Scrutiny was my wake up call. Should there be anymore meanderings I will yank them from their cause. Tramping down the esplanade I called them by their name. 'Deceit and humbuggery' come to mind. If I was without a flaw I would corner them without running, measuring my outcry with these flamboyant others. But for now there are only paradigms with which to brew this solace and I will have come full circle. If others come before me I will take a stance and judging from these others I will reap a great benefit. You might cry out but I will intercede making a mockery of these proceedings. If those that derive satisfaction from such a post don't acquiesce I will be forced to indulge myself in their pandering.

I am walking with my head held high. By whatever means 'they' are close by my side. Sweating and panting I am miles from home and they still haven't let up would mean that the source was not in my computer. Still I was afraid to go home. Being pent up there was no good. I needed to stretch my legs with these demons so close by. And so in my mania I marched on. I was beginning to shout now threatening them with curses. If I was going to endure I would have to employ all of my wit. However these devils were inside my brain and there was no solace that I could bring to bear. Instead 'they' were growing louder. It was clear that they meant to torture me once they had me at a dead end, alone and without allies. I couldn't brook this painful end culminating in great suffering at their hands and so without pause I threw myself beneath a semi-truck screaming semper fidelis! The truck quickly stopped while I was underneath it and I was without so much as a scratch. It seemed that almost immediately the ambulance and police arrived. I merely feigned unconsciousness for a while before I answered their questions. They were, oddly enough, in a chipper mood and I wondered if they, too, were secretly monitoring me as were those from the underworld. In the backcloth I could hear several gunshots being fired. But was I endangering these poor souls? It was too late! I had implicated them in this fateful act.

IV

I was wheeled into the emergency room. More shots rang out and I felt remorse that I might have done these good people wrong. I don't know what kind of injection they administered but I immediately felt pampered and sedated.

Next I was transported upstairs to the floor for the mentally ill. The patients there seemed to be nothing more than impostors. I winked at the nurse to show her my allegiance. However she declined to reciprocate. A strong breed, I thought to myself, a strong ilk indeed! We passed through the protocol of paper work and I was let outside to the patio for a cigarette. There these impostors were milling around, playing their parts like poor actors. This great sham was generating itself with all the force and fraud of coercion. These 'pals' of mine shuffled to and fro impersonating the icon of mental illness. Well, it was plain to see that their deception was for their welfare not mine. I could discern, as could any novice, that their actions and words were premeditated. But I couldn't, for the life of me, tell who was friend and who was foe. Some of them were, no doubt, imitating me while few others appeared to be truly ill. Apparently I was to be held in lock up for attempted suicide. Despite this clientele and any misgivings it felt good to be off the streets where I almost met my end. I was given medication and left alone to sleep. Soon lunch arrived and we all ate in silence. There were no more gunshots and my voices had become muffled. I began to wonder what Ray might think of my situation or especially Claire, my children's book publisher. Were they, too, hounded by these same forces? Were they in danger as well? Either way I could not bring myself to contact them by telephone as of yet and I decided to put correspondence at a later date.

Two days later I was transferred to another floor for good behavior, one might say. There people seemed to be in better shape, capable of conversation and even laughter. More than the other floor we were let out to the deck where we would break the monotony of indoors for fifteen minutes at a time. On a beautiful day this didn't seem to be long enough. The blue sky and puffy clouds had us all enthralled with its great contrast to the gloomy and dingy corridors of the hospital itself.

Five more days passed and I was anxious to depart from this incarceration. I had discovered nothing more of this ominous clatter within these walls and I wondered if things had changed outside as well. As I departed I felt my perceptions sharpened by the light. It would appear that matters had changed for good. But there was something eerie about my surroundings, something inspiring fear from which I didn't know how to rebound. In this queer setting I rushed home seeking out the comfort of my belongings. Then I telephoned Ray to see if there was any news. It seemed as though I had been gone more than a week but the tragedy was still fresh in my mind. However Ray said that not much was happening and I felt relieved that he was safe. It would do no good to tell him all that had happened and so I avoided disclosing to him the bitter news.

Something had happened to me that I

couldn't make sense of and it hadn't disappeared entirely. These portentous moments had me flushed with fear. No, I had never before come this far, to suicide, and I began to grope at the plausible causes for this dilemma. I took my medicine wondering if it was a mere placebo and lay in bed startled by every sound that I heard. It was clear that I was fortunate to be alive but I wasn't out of the woods yet and this fractured my peace of mind. I sat by the window examining my prose and through its transparencies I could feel that my soul was, indeed, sick. Had I come so far only to be dragged down to this muted level of things? For there was this rustling like the sound of bird's wings and these well hidden sirens were reflected in my work?

How would my publishers react if they knew that I was quite ill? It might very

242

well be that they would sunder our relations and as a result I was frightened into hiding the facts at hand. Besides surely things would get better. I was just a little ill disposed for now and this phenomena happening to me would be only like a sneeze, here then gone the next moment. But in the end I wasn't able to convince myself fully and I began to mope over the tragedy which had befallen me.

The days came and went more and more anonymously. I was able to pen a sort of silky gloss here and there but my heart wasn't in it. The matters at hand would sometimes hold me and crippled as such I couldn't see a way out. It seemed that soon these 'others' would be calling for me but I was adamant that they stay their distance and so very artfully I staved off their intrusions begging for more clear insight.

At other times writing was becoming easier and I thought that I was on the verge of something colossal and unexpected. But my brain was occasionally steeped in retribution. Why I could carry a tune or a tear as well as the next man and I had let go of the arrow more than once, I thought to myself. At the same time I bowed and dreamed of faraway places making a mockery of creating. Should I arrive again one fine day at the threshold of these writings i would be enough to sustain me. And so as limpid as the sky I would turn about disinterring the most impossible of propositions.

I began to eat out at various restaurants to save me from my self imposed solitude. Each and every event went by roughly or smoothly but either way I was unscathed. Should my nemesis raise its head I would reply in same? This was my sole reprieve but it didn't come without exceptions. For presently I noticed my sleep was being extirpated by insomnia. Wherever I ate or whatever I imbibed it was becoming the same story. They seemed to be tainting what I ingested with some form of medicine, poisoning me, if you like. With no sleep and a racing mind I traipsed through the town and the parks to spend this exuberance of spirits. These symptoms, good or bad, were my 'rivals' and I couldn't fetch any meaning that I might ascribe to them. With every thought there was distortion and my legs couldn't walk fast enough. Precipitated by, whatever elixir, I was merely a puppet beneath these wishes of the alchemist of this siege. Treated thus my cowardice and repulsion to these forces grew and grew and there was no eluding them.

And so today I walked to see Ray and, what was more, to see if he was somehow implicated in this war of words and poison. He sat in his chair with the look of success and position in life and stood to shake my hand.   Seeing him was a sobering experience.   If he was acting it was consummated with great skill. Meanwhile he reminded me of better times before this so-called 'fall' from the world I once knew. I considered telling him my story but I didn't want to become too reckless in my treatment of these matters. Besides my only two friends were my publishers and I couldn't risk losing their important meaning in my life. I would be left alone to pull out my hair and shout at the moon. He did, however, comment on my appearance asking if I was sleeping alright. I told him quite frankly that I hadn't but I did tell him that I couldn't account for the reasons why. He seemed not to be satisfied with this reply. Perhaps I was acting differently too. I couldn't be sure and he was, after all, quite astute in his study of human behavior. And, to boot, there were my books consider which dealt largely with the cusp of madness. If I didn't watch it I might be looking for a new publisher and editor. Who knows what lay in wait. So as artfully as possible I dismissed myself a little shamefacedly and made tracks back home, jabbering to myself and cursing my good manners. The weight of the world seemed to concuss about me and I couldn't wait to dash out of sight.

In my room it was the same sad story and I began to grow curious about how long it would be that I could fool Ray. I reprimanded myself severely over my indiscretions with him and made a mental note not to visit him until things improved. I was losing touch and my writing was reflecting it. I tossed into the trash sheaves of a manuscript and copious notes no longer wishing to pursue them. I would have to depend on the workings of a censor that hadn't as yet been employed. Before there were changes in the text, of course, but nothing compared to the numberless transgressions of my writing since my 'fall?'

What if I told Ray about my symptoms? Would he be understanding? For it was a business and I wasn't beyond getting fired for such conditions. No, I must write the book that had never seen the light of day. I must engage these devils as in a game of chess and emerge victorious in this chase. Yes, nature was coming apart but it still summoned me. I had fallen before into this trap and I had rebounded successfully. Why couldn't I repeat these same steps, bringing my book to the market with my head held high? It was my only recourse. I had no other alternatives. To write as though my life depended upon it was my only choice. But I laughed out loud at this ultimatum doubting, I suppose, the outcome.

In the meantime I continued to take my medicine wondering still what was actually in it. Suddenly after two days of sleeplessness I turned in for a snooze. Upon awakening some twelve hours later I finally felt relaxed and these mental encumbrances had almost left me altogether. Perhaps my friends and foe had become tired of their mischievous habits and were recoiling from my grasp. Yes I had been unjustly accused and even these specious 'others' realized it by now. Still I didn't give a fig for writing and I spent the day lounging and calling these rabid spirits the pet names that I had given them. Frolicking thus I was once again home. I had finally been spared these indecencies to come forth on my own terms and my invariable charm. It was only a matter of time before I was resurrected and om the public outcry I would be heard from sometime soon. At least I am trying, and not too cavalierly, to mark my paces with well defined relations.

However, I am no longer skating on this thin trail of ice. I have come full circle addressing these underlings, this underworld, without regret. These excursions have cost me dearly but they have made me stronger. Never acquiesce, I say to myself. Perhaps in the future they shall issue a blow from which I can't recuperate but for now there are only resplendent moments left like sunlight in a burning glass.

V

.It is months later and I have departed from my cozy nook and Ray's employment to dwell in a city to the north.

Here these dogged hours clash beyond my understanding. With the rain the darkness has fallen. Nevertheless this November rain pelted down like scattershot as I lay snug in my room, the room that housed a thousand thoughts within me. Sitting thus my nerves began to subside. It was time to roll up my sleeves and get to work. But first I must venture outdoors for coffee where no man is safe. 'Screws, lousy screws,' I paraded for all to hear. I turned on my heels, cap in hand, and rallied toward my cause! I walked with a dapper stride noting that in this dollhouse across the way there lived six children. It was a cottage that stood like a toy house and it was a fine evening punctuated only by crickets. These innocents and fools made for a poor comradery. If only I could fling an epithet and muse beyond this chase. But instead I am ready to spring upon my unfortunate foe. Shall I go mad by their sight? I could, after all, hide from others but not myself. No, at this juncture I couldn't slip away so easily.

As a gentleman passed by I broached his acquaintance. By what surname do you go by? I asked without hesitation. He was quick to reply, 'none of your business, sir!' I couldn't very well insist noticing the common sense of his remark. But I wasn't through with him yet! 'What is this a freak show,'

I hastened, grabbing my sides from laughter, and asking for clemency from these dirty devils. Later, this inwardness must pass like a brief rain. Nevertheless, for now I must incubate my thoughts and come forward bearing the gifts of my words. It is like the light penetrating the sea and mine is to climb the sea of garlands.

Oh, these poor souls that pass my way! Who knows what they are saying about me. I have a sharp eye but I need a little seasoning. I am like an actor without respect for his tools. On the threshold my heart is pounding. What thoughts came into my head, I don't know. But these dirty dogs that lay in slumber mustn't rub me the wrong way or there would be hell to pay. At my expense I can hear the voices growing louder now and these bullies were beating me down with such ferocity that I began to sob. It was as though I was the last man on earth. Even the animals seemed to have deserted me. To top it off there were now more sirens than you could shake a stick at. Time passed and only silence was at my beck and call. It was as though they had their way with me and were no longer anxious to scald me in their fires. But for now I must breathe life into this carcass. What a world! For god's sakes, man, the gentleman next to me has his toenails painted. Meanwhile our bartender is a dry wit , tossing napkins in a sing song fashion for the drinks of all of these unfortunates. But for a few streaks of clouds the sky was magnificent blue and the snow on the distant hills was mother of pearl.

From where I sat lay a delicatessen
and next to it a luggage company. What is
more, above this stood a clock that covered
the entire face of the building. However, it
didn't seem to be working as the dials
hadn't changed since I sat down. Next to
this was a coffee hut. I longed for a coffee
but I didn't dare spend the money, the
money that must come at a more opportune
moment. But I have forgotten to mention
the enormous trees towering above all of us,
their branches breathing splendidly with
the mild breeze at my back. But with this
wretched fever I go into the night. The rites
of men have fallen upon me. Shall I
disencumber the tripe of these ages, ages
meant for no man before me? To this I say
curses. By god, I was a man of great mettle.
But I should stop moping and wipe away

the tears. We were, after all, so close that I heard their voices in my own. A feud was looming on the horizon. That much was sure and certain. And, believe you me, I promise to tear them limb from limb in this row. In the meantime I am swept away with ennui, troubled and forsaken and ragged. Shall I rise to the occasion? Why, of course! Though the wind crept through the windows like a fire and there was no stopping it. And the wind can be so eerie, so terribly eerie!

I wasn't exactly an intellect suffering from gigantism but I was still aware of extraordinary skills. This I observed at a cemetery where I sat down as though grieving a loved one. My thoughts turned to when I was a young man. I remembered standing in the doorway one fine evening renouncing my past for a more conciliatory present and I began to grow tentacles of an author dispossessed by all and every means. I heard the calls of every man who laid me down in word or deed and I no longer succored the privileges of those about me. Oh, but I was having an involuntary relapse now and I was sick to my stomach. I began to wrench; vomiting over the tombstones I sat by. It must have been the water I consumed and a bad case of nerves but I passed more, it seemed, than I had imbibed. However, I felt better after this evacuation and I arose resurrected to tip my hat and to smile among my colleagues.

Walking toward home I feel at the top of my form even though these well-wishers smack of insincerity. I tried to write but I wasn't pleased with the words, any of them, and the alabaster throat of my revelations was holding me down without exception. Outside the flower pots were warmed by the sun and there were dogs barking. They sounded strange to my ears and so I crept downstairs to observe. It would seem that the commotion at the toy house was responsible for the yelping dogs and I returned to my desk thinking that in creation one can do whatever he wishes. So my verse was flat. It was no more than a minor obstacle in my path. Besides one must believe in something. There is no other choice. Merely lift your spoon and a value comes to the fore. I was worth my salt and I would, no doubt, emerge the victor. It had been a long road and even though fate was running me ragged I was still on my uppers. I was not just a bundle of knots and the bridge to my awakening, I felt, was very near.

Take away as if you saw fit the breach of this madness.   Whatever I pursue, sometimes, leaks into my brain with exquisite precision.   Other times I wasn't worth a good scolding.   However, if I am nudged at the cornerstones of my mind, envious of those that went before me, I might one day soon reach a clearing in which my efforts would be exonerated.

Down Coolcrest Avenue I wandered. Followed?   Why of course!   Happening upon a bum in the street begging I closed in upon him.   As I only had a coin on my person I asked him if he would like a cigarette.   At this he perked up and I began to roll some tobacco.   Feigning mental illness he carried on not waiting for any response to his gibberish.   But as I lit his cigarette I promptly asked him if he was a Cherokee by chance.   I didn't know what I was getting at but it appeared to be the right thing to say. I wasn't altogether happy with his poor manners but I, myself, wasn't proud of my own. Perhaps we were both kin in this matter. Oh, but he was a stronger man than I. Colder, lonelier, he straddled the saddle better than most. So, in the next trip, I made sure of giving him my sleeping bag. Something, anything, to alleviate the cold and abominable pain which we could all do something about. It no longer mattered who he was, friend or foe something of which I wasn't certain. Besides, I had no interest in this game of words spoken to oneself. I had suffered it again and again myself.

It was winter now and I have been evicted. The cold that embraced one translated into the meager necessities offered by the Red Cross, or the church, or the county food lines. The county thrift store that had a sign for part-time work some time ago now entertained my mind. Surely they would see that I was an honest and decent prospect for such employment. I would work more cheaply than any others and I was congenial as well.

And so I walked down Fifth Avenue to the location of the thrift store. But first, on the way, I stopped at a gas station restroom to wash my face and to comb my hair. Staring into the mirror I caught a glimpse of a man I no longer knew. Practicing parsimony I hadn't shaved recently and sporting a beard made me look ten times older. But nothing, as of yet, could be done about it. I would have to sell myself as I stood.

I entered the store run by a few elderly women. They seemed from the outset to be

261

endeared to me. No doubt my shyness seemed to entrap them though I was not just a little ashamed of myself and my appearance. Well, they had taken to me and I was rewarded with a job. My main business would be to shelf books in their proper place. It was a breeze and we began each day with free coffee and donuts. Little did they know that for now it was my only meal for the day. And, of course, there was the godsend of a small room in the back where I could lay my body down.

Things were running smoothly, super as a matter of fact. Food from a nearby shelter house and a roof over my head were now generously offered and I couldn't very well refuse these commodities. To top it off my book was soon to be consummated and I was ecstatic as a writer must be. It was like a sibling to myself glowing in the darkness and I pressed these words to my chest welcoming the approval of their substance. All in all it was a fine dream and better in many ways to my last haunt. I was free!

My first treat to myself were razor blades and being clean shaven halved my age. My employers were quick to notice the positive changes. I could do no wrong in their eyes and with Christmas approaching I managed to scrap up enough money to buy them candles for the holidays. Now I was glistening in the winter's sun with a safe place to sleep and a hot plate at my disposal. However, while these nannies for employers were quite kind to me there still existed the onerous presence, a deep and saturated solitude among these warring tribes that I couldn't entirely shake off. But my novel was now close to its conclusion

and nothing could stop me shy of a miracle.
Had I not carried to the logical end the story
of my travels?

VI

I was dozing now but, all of a sudden,
I snapped to! Awakening from this sound
sleep I dashed downstairs to the thrift shop
running a little late for my shift. It was a
day like any other, I suppose, and yet there
was something different about it. I could
swear that my usual entourage had all but
disappeared. No longer was I hounded by
these devils that had interfered with my life.
However, my writing was suffering at the
same time. I would sit for long periods
gazing at those who walked by me but
without the alarm by which they had

formerly seized me. I wondered how on earth they had so patently expressed themselves in the past and presently so quickly disappeared. This was a godsend and I welcomed it with open arms. How could I have fallen for this trap? I no longer knew but, equally, I was frightened by their return. As it was Christmas time now everyone in the office was sharing their mirth. I found myself not just a little giddy for this yuletide. No, I was wildly ecstatic and my exuberance spilled over into my everyday affairs. Even the management offered me praise saying what I never truly knew, that my depression was absent and that my spirits had picked up. This was much to their pleasure. Perhaps these demons had disappeared for some reason with the holidays and they would reappear afterwards. But these moments of doubt were short-lived and any opposition seemed to have vanished for good.

Sometimes I appeared to be the life of the party, drinking eggnog and toasting to everyone's good health. I had been given a small tree and I invited those around me to decorate it. I was no longer churlishly rude nor ill tempered, no longer dismal and irritable with others. You could say that I had been born again and you wouldn't be far from the truth. But then it happened! It was Christmas day and the shop was not open. There was not a soul on the streets that I took to walking. It was an ominous and dreadful feeling as though I had been abandoned. Not only were the devils not about but the friends that I had made were similarly absent. It was as though I was the last man on earth. A stray dog was the only companion that I had. And so with good spirits I took him home and fixed him something to eat. His tail never stopped wagging and we quickly became soul mates. I had never before had a pet and I was delighted with his company. I didn't know how the landlady would react and I didn't know if I could give him up to the dog pound if she was against his presence. Yes, we had a lot in common, vagabonds, so to speak, and usually happy beneath all appearances. I was almost willing to give up my apartment if the landlady couldn't shine upon him favorably. At least we would have each other for a few of the holidays before the workers returned. It must be mentioned that some of the employers had asked me over to share a meal but I refused feeling a little out of sorts. Perhaps this meeting with the dog was fated upon me by the powers that be. I seemed to recall a dog leash at the thrift shop that I might procure as well as dog bowls for our future plans.

We slept together that night frolicking with each others attention. Both of us were formerly homeless and hungry, both of us a little weary and starved for affection. However, just as suddenly as we had befriended one another we were separated. For taking a walk the next morning the dog chased a cat across the street and before I could get to him a car struck him and sped off into the distance. I was beside myself with grief. He only managed to crawl to the curb before he expired. He didn't stand a chance. I had cried out to him but in vain and now everything came reeling back to me. Who was the perpetrator of this crime and why hadn't he stopped? It appeared that I had become all too comfortable with these seemingly harmless gadabouts surrounding me. Now every stitch of this entourage grew wild by my side. It was impossible to deny their presence. They were now everywhere! Henceforth I became more suspicious of my work cronies as well. No doubt I would be struck someday like the nameless dog that I had befriended. "Kill me now," I screamed, livid with the onlookers congregating by the dog. That night beneath the lonely moon I scampered up the highway ferreting out any and all visitants that broached me. You who cry out, I muttered, let it be known that I have suffered all manner of things. The only man that I truly trusted was, perhaps, a bum on the street whom had nothing left to lose. Tomorrow I would make a gesture of friendship that he couldn't refuse. A simple cup of coffee would be in order and together we would pledge a good and great friendship. About this I was adamant!

Oh, but my mind was still spinning with the memory of the dog that lay there inert and stone dead. It broke my heart and sent me to reexamining my surroundings once more but this time with finality. I would, I must, once and for all take these seeming innocents to justice. I would no longer be trampled by their foul logistics nor would I run amok and get arrested for deeds better left unsaid.

By Spring I had come full circle. I trusted nobody, not even myself. As a result my relations were suffering but I couldn't put it behind me. The image of this dead dog was still upon me and all of my perceptions grew from this image.

Somebody had taken the felicity that was once mine and murdered it. They had left me with a few hard truths and nothing more. It would take a new book and a good work ethic to evade the substance of these devils all about me. And so I took up my pen once again prepared for any mischief that might come my way. It had been a month since I had written a page; lulled into a false sense of security by these impostors, I suppose. But I was pleased with where I had left off and I, in fact, continued from these pages, pages that seemed as fresh as linen. No, I had been deceived and hoodwinked by this marginalia of safety and good tidings. No longer would I possess good manners when it came to these pristine images laid down by steadfast rules. Inside I felt as though I could go on and on with great responsibility. In a sense

I was more free than I had ever been. Should my acquaintances become too much I would simply move on and live the life of the fox. After all there must be someplace for the likes of me. If not among men, well then, among the animals and the woods.

Meanwhile I pressed on oblivious of these hurdles. My occupation of writing was taking hold and I couldn't forsaken these words with those of taller men. If one tries to remember he can recite, off the cuff, those that befriended him as well as those that did not. But what of this skirl piping the notes of solitude. It was time, my time, to depart what was once halcyon in my blood. Where I would go was not certain but I was sure to find the ilk by which I had come upon these lodgings. Yes, I must move on though a little unsteady on my feet. So briefly we departed with one another, wishing each other luck and good fortune. I almost took to weeping feeling something wasn't right but I abstained calling upon my courage.

The nights and days passed. I felt that I was growing old before my time. The dreams that I held onto were now becoming invisible and I didn't know how to retrieve them. Nevertheless I moved forward and with my savings I managed to eat and to hold a mailbox for correspondence entirely given up to publishing houses. Soon, one far cry in the distance, I was the recipient of good news. I had captured the interest of a publisher. It came without too much coaxing and I was ecstatic about this invitation. If I sold another book I might very well be in good standing.

As fate dictated I was accepted and my dreams were again becoming true. On this fair day I roamed without equal. I was the object of tall tales and poems of my heart. I had captured their attention! It was pennies on the dollar but I wasn't worth anything more, I supposed. Anything, anything would move my soul. Why it, my writing, had been full of such deceit and still I was awakening to this newborn clinic of words. The burst of these rhymes had me coming and going. The struggle and tenacity that follows me has driven me to succeed in each and every way. But I had been groomed to no more and no more would I say. Helpless, oh my helplessness, please honor a man of such deliberations that he could no longer see straight. Please ransack these tributaries of my brain. For all purposes I am deceased. Should I be accepted to this elite club, again, I would holler no more. I would wag my tail. After all I am a nuisance with which to be dealt.

What is the philosophy of these devils? For meanwhile I swung from the highest branches while the blackness strolled in from the darkling skies. Please sketch my face for I am without a mirror to do justice to this faltering image. Drum when you are ready my darlings and you will find me satisfied merely by your call. Let the arrow fly. There will be no more chase. So I am on the run, nonetheless, I am bereft of the troublesome climes.

Perhaps I should not have given away my sleeping bag but it was a noble effort and I found myself proud of my actions. I was once what this bum was about. Now it seemed so long ago when I was invincible, when I could have my way with any woman, when writing was a holiday and I swam the channel without difficulty. So bitter and so sweet I was then the master of my domain. Now I was plagued but still I had this great story. Spring was well upon me.   Unlike usual it was an inclement season, one given to severe cold and flowers blossoming late. I was at a hovel across from the bank.   Sweeping floors and cleaning restrooms at a library I shelved books as well. The devils had me coming and going. However, without them, oddly enough, I had next to nothing. Soon I was tired of this mechanical form of employment. I took to writing now with renewed interest though despair enveloped me. Without a moment's thought I pawned my father's ring. With this transgression tears ran down my cheeks and my eyes smarted. I was without resources leaving work for the risk of writing.

My misery was growing day by day

but I had drafted a piece of work that seemed unassailable by any means. Surely this creation would find a publisher and my luck would turn. And so with only a pittance left, a few dull coins, I posted a query letter to a publishing house. A few weeks later, to my astonishment, I discovered a promising reply asking to see my manuscript. I was at my wits' end and not above stealing for this correspondence to be sent. But first I would try to sell a few of my favorite books for the appropriate funds.

I sat on a bench at the park with my meager belongings and propositioned one after the other. Fortunately the time came when a generous soul wandered my way. Realizing my poverty he handed me quite a sum without taking the books or other paraphernalia. It was enough to eat a few meals and to post my book. I thanked him profusely and scurried off to mail my manuscript.

I was staying at a shelter for the homeless now and out of the spring rain and cold. With food in my stomach time seemed to pass most graciously. A flood of expectations seemed to flourish in my obsessive mind. Finally, one fine day, I received a note of interest in publishing my book. Well, I was beside myself with joy and I promptly showed this bit of news to one of the caregivers at the shelter. With the proof of the letter I was able to obtain a few dollars for food. He was adamant about my returning the money but wished me good luck with this gesture for which I was eternally grateful.

Time seemed to stand still! But with due haste I suppose the publisher was giving it his all and in this connection I finally heard from him. A kinder letter I had never received. He was as exuberant about my work as was I. I had finally snagged a good prospect and promises were offered to accommodate me financially.

It was a cloudless sky that reflected my mood. The publisher, Keith, was sympathetic to my plight and offered me traveling expenses so that we might work feverishly upon my book and its editing. I was excited and overwhelmed, ecstatic beyond memory but for Ray and his former generosity.

And so, the next day, I boarded the bus to take to his place of business about one hundred miles northbound. Flushed with anxiety I arrived a few hours later. Those about me seemed to be fraught with worry. No doubt this was because of my success at flushing my poor opponents out of their lairs. My document would see to it that they were no longer invisible. It would see to it that this secret society could not last. Perhaps I had banished them altogether. It would seem as though I had them all running like gazelles. In the meantime I had finally discovered, again, somebody that gave to me credibility in my task of writing.

Arriving at the address given me I tipped my hat to whom, I thought, was the gardener. As it turned out it was Keith and he shook my hand like a long lost friend. Apparently this was his own brand of therapy, snipping at the overgrown bushes and flowers. Of course, in our conversation, there was no mention of mental illness with which to intimidate me. Perhaps this was

because I had offered him the commentary
that my writing was done, in part, through
the conversations that I had with a bum at
the park. In this way I managed to escape
any ridicule about my little creation and its
sources. If he was involved somehow
without my knowing it I would do well to
keep him at bay permitting us to mirror one
another with some deceit. Anyway, there
seemed to be a hush in the air that allowed
me clear thoughts. If I was to venture a
guess I would wager that he was on my
side if, indeed, he knew anything at all
about my endeavors and their first handed
nature. Still, perhaps, it was a dead
giveaway that I dissimulate these
circumstances by inventing the picture of a
bum assisting me; especially since my
clothes were tattered and I had next to no
luggage with me. This didn't seem to

deduct from his respectful attention. No doubt if he truly knew who or what I was about he might very well be even more deferential in our dealings. But, all in all, his actions and decorum were more than satisfactory and I looked forward to editing my book with him without any reservations.

In addition to his other attributes he offered me a place to stay at his guest house. I told him that I didn't wish to put him out but that I would prefer this to a hotel. He was quick to agree with me and after dinner, which we took at a nearby restaurant, we arrived at his home to continue working on my manuscript.

After one week of working tirelessly upon my novel and getting along famously he broached me with an offer that I couldn't refuse. Understanding that I was now without a home or work he asked me if I would be interested in staying at his guest house while gardening and, ironically enough, helping him to send out rejection notices. Well, I couldn't say no. It was the perfect arrangement. Besides it would take some time before my book was released and he was willing to give to me some advanced wages as well as a small salary for helping him out. A better friend one couldn't meet!

Gardening at his home and office suited me well. However, sending rejection notices struck me the wrong way. It held too many memories of my own dismissals of the past. Still it was a far cry from my employment at the thrift store and elsewhere and I took it upon myself to let Keith know of my appreciation with haste. Keith was, it turned out, a strong successful character. His wife and child had died in an automobile accident but still he was able to rebound from this horror. I felt sorrow for him and his plight and I tried to alleviate the pain with a few well chosen words and gestures. Occasionally I would take him out for a meal or to a movie against his advice to save my money. But I never had that much desire to scrimp and to save and it seemed like the honorable thing to do. Besides, the truth be known, his company was a welcome change from my past isolation.

Months passed by me and as there was little work remaining with my first novel given to him I began drafting plans for my second one with, of course, constant counsel from Keith on its progress. I suppose that after his loss of family he had thrown himself into more and more work to diminish the pain. Yes, despite his loss he had maintained a fine sense of humor which endeared him to me more than ever. No, my own problems paled to his and I was thankful for his kindness. He was doubtless filled with empathy for me as well.

And so well into the year I had eventually made claim to my second tale. Unlike my other books that dealt with a steep form of inwardness I took it upon myself to write about a physician and the reunion with his family. Loosely based upon my father I found it to be not in the least difficult to express. My memories were so keen and abundant that it wrote itself. On top of this Keith found it quite memorable and we would often parley with its content assuming its different roles, miming the characters with great joy.

Meanwhile those 'others' irritable

about me seemed to be running away one after the other. Most probably this was the result of my new ally, Keith. At least, at this point in time, that was the way I understood it. His alliance had scared them away like a bevy of birds. In other words his medicine was too strong for their shenanigans whatever they might be.

But soon there was to be an office party at Keith's home. This tended to make me nervous as everyone would be with their family and friends. Hence many strangers would be asking too many questions about my position in life and I would have my head on the chopping block. Keith sensed my discomfort and tried to put me at ease. But it was too late. The past had come reeling back to me and all of the manifold problems of the chase. And so as the hour approached I ducked out the back way, trying to distance myself from the party and any passers-by with ulterior motives.

I ended up in a café drinking coffee. Here I imagined the guest house and the strangers that were now upon my residence. Would they enter it and discover my personal notes and my second novel? Would they, at this moment, be talking about what a queer fellow I was and how something was very wrong with me? Nonetheless, it felt good to be out of their reach. In time I would return home with ample excuses for my disappearance. Perhaps I could invent something so momentous that I would catch them all off guard. It must, I reminded myself, be done with good taste. Nothing so severe as a death but nothing too light not to demand my presence. That is it, I thought. Thus I would posit a previous date made with her and her very own fear of crowds. I would blame it all on this fictitious person and her irrational fears and, furthermore, I would express my sorrow about being away. With the proper touch I would align myself with the present company swearing off anymore such trysts. Yes, I would paint the picture of an unreasoning and absurd seduction with a woman who was both beguiling and unsound. But would I be able to convince Keith of these copious lies? He seemed to wink at me with a good natured pat on the back. After all, he had read my books and therefore knew of such deceit.

One woman at the party seemed to take a deep interest in me telling me of her respect for my first book with this firm. I felt suddenly not a little ashamed of it and I simply told her that I had tried. To this she

288

objected saying that it was a fine, fine piece of work. Then she asked me if I had more coming. I told her 'yes' reluctantly but lied saying that it wasn't ready as of yet. After all I didn't want to give myself away completely with these very personal works and to add to this, perhaps unwisely, I abhorred her meddling. Yes, these works were my siblings and I was touchy about those who knew me personally and those that knew me from my books alone. She seemed a little nonplussed about my answers to her questions. She kept on digging and digging bent on finding out more about me as if I was her project or a pet that she wished to domesticate. Meanwhile the clamor of the crowd began to diminish before despair got the best of me. After giving me the third degree my bitterness toward her probe began to fade and I dismissed myself from anymore of her rant. Who cared if to her I lacked candor. If she was playing the aesthete why should I be responsible for her rather harsh companionship?

In my guest house I scribbled like a monk with scripture. Surely these wounds given me by her interrogation was unforeseen by Keith. My healthier impulses were now growing but the twilight began to consume me. I was becoming possessed by the sacred and the profane. That night I had a dreamless sleep beneath a sky thickset with stars.

The next morning I prepared to go to work at the office. I wondered if Keith would rebuke me in any way for having disappeared before his party ended. However, as usual he was kind enough to ignore it. After all we nearly lived beneath the same roof. While speaking about the night before I made mention, off the cuff so to speak, about the spitefulness I felt from the woman whom had interrogated me without the least apology. He happened to have noticed her and second guessed her surly business. However we changed the subject shortly having said enough.

Still I wasn't entirely without any misgivings and I wondered secretly about what part she played in this apparent chase. But for what guidance was I searching. I reminded myself to keep an eye out and nothing more. To thrust myself into the subject of this ostensible chase I must employ great discretion, I sighed. It wouldn't do to threaten all of Keith's good deeds with presuppositions that were damaging to our peace of mind, as in the case with Ray. If 'she,' Deborah, and I were to meet again I would merely look her straight up and down but otherwise without a trace of finding fault with her. This was how I would support myself, playing absent-minded and playing the blockhead. With but a glance I would search for any incriminating evidence. I would find it unnecessary to refute her prattle and I would bow out graciously from any confrontation. As it turned out she seemed to give to me the cold shoulder in the hallway no doubt put off with last night's obtuse performance on my part. Well it wasn't up to me to kiss her brow, I thought, and I acted as though nothing contrary had happened.

But today it was warm out and I was as happy as a doe in the sun. I was grooming the bushes with tender loving care. I was no longer worried about what arguments one or the other had against me. So oblivious had I become that I felt as though I was sleep walking and I whistled a merry tune.

VII

The days have since passed unremarkably and my book has been published. According to Keith it was time that I took on some additional chores, that is, the chore of signing my book at various locations. In this way publicity and sales would pick up. He, no doubted, could see me shake from this proposal but he nevertheless considered it mandatory if I wanted to pursue any further publication. It was a business after all. And who knows, he said, perhaps I would find it an amusing past time, one that would rally me toward my pause. It would take me more than butterflies not to succumb to this invitation. After all a part of me was soaring like a child in the heavens.

And so upon this day I presented myself to a local bookstore bent on persuading the public to read my book. It was quite a jolt for me to see it on the shelves. As before it was humbling but uplifting at the same time. People seemed to take delight in my signature and time passed without any of the fretfulness that I prepossessed. So this, again, was the writer's life, I reflected. It appealed to me more than the last time. Of course if the question arose as to how I had invented this tale I would express my gratitude, as before, to a homeless person I had met along the way. In this way I would see to it, as I have said, that I was one remove from the creation that was so very personal. But it didn't take me long before I grew suspicious of some of the patrons. Some, it seemed, were insistent about disinterring my experiences and the folklore that I had knitted about the so-called sirens. Were they, perhaps, wary suspecting first hand exposure? Were they, in part, responsible for the content I alone had created? Were some of them present at the original sites that I had traveled? Again, the history of the chase rose its unseemly head. Sometimes, I must admit, I struggled for the right words to ay. However, I was merely a ghost writer; presumably the tale took its roots in another. At times this fictitious arrangement seemed like an insult. I found it difficult to hold back from the truth. The truth, that is, of being the sole creator and

295

my remarks were desultory at best. At the end of a long day I would clamber up the steps to my guest house a little worn out from keeping on my toes. Nonetheless I was satisfied with my performance and Keith, as well, was congratulatory toward the efforts and strides he witnessed in his visit with me.

Each visit to a store was much like another. I was becoming fluent in my gibberish about the main character and because of my proper packaging and keen marketing skills on the cover of my book sales seemed to be increasing dramatically. At home I was anxious about completing another book. Why should I stop with this little success? It seemed as though I was coming into my own. Thus I would make a calendar to which I would remain faithful on the progress of my book. However at times it was like forcing a lock and my mind seemed to stall at anymore composition. Still things were running smoothly despite these encumbrances and I would often share, perhaps prematurely, a part of the text with Keith. I could almost do no wrong. He was startled at my progress and encouraged me to no end.

The truth be known I missed my gardening with these signings and I longed for my former agenda. But I pledged to the forces that be that I would continue on in this same vein and that I wouldn't be smitten by this fever to write alone and forsake the signings. Nonetheless, like it or not, I found my mind was faltering and steeped in a newborn silence and in this fog I began to become discouraged. At least with the consummation of this new book I wouldn't have to hide from the reader, inventing the story of ghostwriting.

Oh, but these signings began to cripple me. My nerves were shot. I could barely go on and in this stupor I longed for completion of this publicity. My routine had dragged me down and I felt that I could no longer be responsible for this poke at self aggrandizement. No, I could no longer play the hero of these words, basking in the light of success. Instead I was taken aback to the origins that first provoked me to write. In this light I could see now that the truth of these words rang out once again. I could see that I was, indeed, not the writer of tall tales nor ghostwriting but the architect of truths about being subjected to a form of uncanny surveillance and to a chase that I didn't understand. Surely others had come and gone in this same frenzy and were never heard from again. Would I persevere or succumb to these devils that seemed to surround me at the bookstores. It would seem that the stage was set and, once again, I was the recipient of poor manners and thought interference. Together they had trailed me to the ends of the earth and were untiring in their pursuit of me though I was still uncertain of their object.

Nevertheless I wasn't fond of becoming homeless again and yet, what could I say, this entire affair was becoming too much for me. I was fuming with anger. Wherever I held up they were sure to be. No matter what strides I made they were forever by my side, nudging me this way and that way, until I lost all perspective. And, oh, what dread was being stirred up by these warriors of the spirit. I tell you this madness must cease before we are all taken by a tether to our end. Perhaps I was the first such man, an experiment if you will, of sound waves and telepathy and clairvoyance of sorts. Why having no family of my own I was the perfect victim for this chase.

The last and most unnerving aspect of this time was my growing mistrust of Keith. He seemed to, of a sudden, be running me ragged with chores and propositions. Nevertheless, I befriended him just the same and I told myself if he was against me I could no longer go on. But fate had grabbed me by the collar and was dragging me down. I needed a new ally, one who wouldn't expect so much of me. And so on the pretext of merely going out to dinner to toast our success I broached him about my future plans and the fatigue that was setting in. Well, he didn't want to hear about it and for the first time he became my employer, stern and expectant. No longer sympathetic toward my plight he now pressed home with an itinerary that was quite objectionable and I told him so. The rest of the evening was spoiled and we remained taciturn until we said good night. In the stark night I tossed and turned, obsessed with a new plan. There was no mistaking it I had shown my true colors and I was being reprimanded for it. I suddenly turned on Keith as though he was now an adversary. My head was sick with worry. I was about to lose my home and my job as well. Meanwhile these miscreants in the backcloth were growing wild with each moment. I was staggering with disbelief and insomnia and I couldn't conceive of a clearing where all would be right again. I was miserable but no tears came. I was locked up into myself but no amount of effort could conceal my grief. I felt as though I was living another's life and without consolation my mind raced on without me.

I had hardly slept a wink when the alarm went off. Like it or not change, drastic change, was coming and to boot Keith was rubbing my nose in it. Without compromising myself I must speak earnestly to him and depart. As it turned out I wasn't making much out of nothing for Keith had driven to the office without me. My feelings were being sacrificed and if it wasn't for the money that he owed me I would have bolted without saying good bye.

I packed the one bag with which I had arrived and with some sorrow scurried to the office. By the time I reached the publishing house Keith's mood had swung around. The office seemed uncommonly quiet. Evidently he felt that he had punished me enough. To my astonishment after having wreaked havoc with my soul he offered me another home. Perhaps, he said, we merely got off on the wrong foot. As I had nowhere to go, and it was quite apparent that the forces of evil surrounded me, I consented. Later, upon meeting my new landlord, I was taken in by his cunning. I don't know what on earth Keith might have said to this gentleman, Daniel, but he seemed to treat me with kid gloves as had Keith originally. It would appear that I continue on in my same vein but that I take two weeks off to get my nerves together. By now I was physically ill and I agreed that I would take a train seaside for a holiday. Ah, the notion of baking in the sun and swimming the waters was the sensible and practical thing to do. I couldn't remember the last time that I had a vacation. Meanwhile I felt that the entire world was awake and digging its claws into me.

As I left Keith to go with Daniel to his home I merely said 'watch your backside' thinking that I owed him the warning. He seemed to turn abruptly toward me with a quizzical look. Unfortunately, we didn't see eye to eye but the damage had been done and as we boarded his car I waved at Keith's reflection in the glass door. I wondered what new ventures were awaiting me at Daniels and if I would wear him down as presumably I had Keith.

His house seemed common enough and my room had a shower. That night after a long deserved nap we had a barbecue and I found myself chatting with him into the wee hours of the morning. Tomorrow I would make travel arrangements for the sea and Daniel would give me a lift. Suddenly it all seemed so simple!

Heading southward toward the coast I began to feel some shame in rocking the boat with Keith. Suddenly I felt thankful for his gestures of kindness and I made a mental note of returning some sort of favor to undo what had been done. Had I sold my soul to these devils? But no sooner had I thought this when I began feeling out of my element and preoccupied with some of these companions of travel. Again doubt began to rush in. The urgency brought about, perhaps from being alone, began to ransack my nerves. I felt like a beaten man on a beaten path. I decided to send to Keith and Daniel postcards no matter what the fates conspired. What could be said but that, on the one hand, I was filled with wonder, while on the other, I was being duped, almost drugged by these same apparitions that with great interest swam by me. But my heavens how far had I come in the recent past published and with a home address. Certainly no matter what peril lay before me I had once vanquished fears and come out ahead of this ruthless game. Why not now? Why should matters be so difficult? Of all of the dreams that were mine hadn't a good portion of them come true?

From the shore by my hotel I took to the sea where the waves would console me. I was growing tired of this lonely regimen never truly quenching my thirst for love. What of these seeming adversaries so brutal and filled with discontent? What species was I always aborting, this species of love? Oh, but the waters were giving me a sense of freedom and whomever 'they' were didn't bother me in the least.

That night almost able to touch the moon romance, as they say, was in the air. Dancing and laughter seemed to be everywhere, lifting me out of my bilious and ill-tempered self. It was truly like some form of magnetism and allurement which had been foreign to me up to now. Years ago I had fallen in love and it turned out badly. So much so that I had tried to replace it by other means. Not long after that, come to think of it, was the advent of all of these menacing others.

But presently I found myself dancing with one that had the eyes of love. My sorrows were absent and I longed for a new life. Neither as an artist nor a vagabond, mind you, but endeared to this woman in such a way as to be the erasure of all of this past deceit. My stay with Keith, my books, and Ray seemed to me like a bad dream. No longer was I destitute nor hungry for success. I wanted to be free of these ill-begotten roles and to live for pleasure alone. All of this dawned on in a sheer moment. I felt happiness rain down upon me without end. Yes, for the first time in many years I was truly coming into my own.

And so whirling with the music beneath a full moon we danced again and again unable to get enough of it. Later we would dine and toast to our health. Her charms were limitless and she didn't seem to care about what I did for a living. It was enough that we were together! I told myself that if one was truly in love with another this love couldn't be refused nor traded for anything. It was with this credo that I pursued her, Colleen, sparing no signs of affection. I felt ashamed of my little art work in the face of this happiness. It had taken such a toll on me. Myself, the solo artist, churlish and unforgiving. I had enough of this to last a lifetime. It was strange, too, that this meeting had so closely coincided with the act that I had shorn my hair and shaved my beard. It was as though I was coming out of seclusion again. It was the type of withdrawal that shields one from living life and succoring the glad flowers of happiness. I felt ages younger and as though the child in me had finally awoken. I would never write another word and I felt like I had finally banished a curse. Still it was a curse that had seen me through madness, homelessness, and hunger. But this creativity had been hopelessly married to insolence and conceit and Colleen would probably not recognize me from my writings. In them I was imprisoned from the beginning to the end.

Laying with Colleen in the wee hours of the morning I wept like a child, unafraid of her rejection, and swore against my previous life up and down. Well, the cleansing had taken place and now we were both ready to bathe in the sea. There, spewing water from our lips, we laughed and giggled like children. Then on the shore beneath an umbrella we combed one another's hair and watched the seagulls looking like statuary, staring silently out to sea. If anyone had proposed such a tryst I wouldn't have believed it. But now I sat a new man no longer afraid of my feelings. To this end I scribbled a few notes to Keith about the metamorphosis of my life and told him that I wouldn't be returning.

Where would I go? With Colleen, of course. We had both struck such a chord as to make some preparations for living together. What would I do? Anything but write, I scowled.

When we first met Colleen had come to me saying that she was struck with my soft spoken manner. From the very outset she had chosen me and seen through me as only a woman could. What if I was never to be lonely again! In human terms I was being resurrected but I couldn't, as in my past, be cynical about these affairs. No, I would shower her with love and the trinkets of love. If, at times, I feared that I would awaken without her, well, this was only natural. After all having shared in such glory was almost foreign to my past.

While I said nothing about being a

published author she wasn't so reticent about her livelihood - life on a farm! Apparently she had taken over this piece of real estate after her parent's death. Though she wasn't entirely alone (she had a few workman who lived on the premises) nevertheless she lived by herself working night and day. She was quite buxom and the epitome of good health. Good humor and giddiness were among her strongest attributes and she never failed to be a good listener. Though why she had such attentive ears for me was beyond my comprehension.

Since her appearance I had lost my fatal entourage. There was not a trace of anyone bearing arms against me. Finally now I could breathe. I had aborted all of my many misadventures. With her intensity and strengths she was like the ultimate ally. With her lay none of the anathema of my scabrous excursions. I felt as though I had cheated death. Complete calm enveloped me and it didn't occur to me that our plans were premature. All that I could say about my past with any certainty was that I never completely gave up. As regarding Colleen I, of course, wondered why she had never married. However, I assumed from our conversation that her parents and she were very close and in the years of their illnesses they depended heavily upon her care.

This proposal of living on a farm intrigued me to no end. She spoke with such love of the animals and small crops that I could easily imagine myself there lending a helping hand. With my correspondence with Keith I could very well give him the address by which I could be reached with any earnings, wages, and royalties from my book sales. Happily I could venture forth with not only my labor but with a little money as well.

It must be said that I marveled again and again at the beatings I had taken and still survived. But what were my deceptions now? I had none! My feelings for Colleen were delicate but profound and irrevocable. I had arisen from the dust to pardon myself for any and all of my misgivings. Whatever my shortcomings I would make up for with hard work, work that demanded physical labor without any of the mental agitation I formerly knew too well. Toward my abilities she was so flattering that I was becoming the caricature of the farm hand. I had to laugh at these intimacies. However, I was truly acquiring a self image corpulent with good sense. It was labor with dignity and not the contemptuous position that I held as a novelist. With great delight I was brimming with these new forces at work. Merely to conceive of them shook me to the core. My god, man, I was being filled with the heavens! Two weeks after my arrival here, my life being changed so dramatically, we both boarded the train destined for my new home. Beneath me I could feel the rails. Yes, up to now I had lived a false life, one given to irrational outbursts and flamboyancy. I was pedaling my wares to publishing houses that I truly didn't give a fig for. All of the query letters, the trials and tribulations of my efforts, were worth nothing. Almost over night I had become a man. Whatever makes the world go around is none of my business. While all the world was sleeping I was to be, after all is said and done, a simple and happy farmer!

Epilogue

One year later

I arrived in town with no more than a satchel and a sleeping bag. I would suppose that it was no less nor more than any other sleepy seaside town. However, it seemed from the outset to; perhaps, garnish the promises of being a writer.

January 2008
Santa Rosa, CA

www.ingramcontent.com/pod-product-compliance
Lightning Source LLC
Chambersburg PA
CBHW050108280326
41933CB00010B/1012